Digital Strategy Framework

Digital Strategy Framework

A Practical Guide for Business Incumbents

Amit Prabhu

BUSINESS EXPERT PRESS

Leader in applied, concise business books

Digital Strategy Framework: A Practical Guide for Business Incumbents

First published in 2024 by
Business Expert Press, LLC
222 East 46th Street, New York, NY 10017
www.businessexpertpress.com

ISBN-13: 978-1-63742-565-7 (paperback)
ISBN-13: 978-1-63742-566-4 (e-book)

Business Expert Press Big Data, Business Analytics, and Smart Technology Collection

First edition: 2024

10 9 8 7 6 5 4 3 2 1

To my wife, Devashri, and my son, Achintya, for your invaluable support throughout the book writing journey

Description

Most of the global incumbents have embarked on the digital transformation journey. But only a few have a clear direction of where they are heading and what they are doing. Some of them rush through the transformation too fast. As a result, they miss out on some critical steps. Some of them move too slowly. As a result, they are late to the market than their competitors. As per a recent study by McKinsey, 70 percent of digital transformation projects fail. A large portion of this 70 percent comprises the incumbents. There are several reasons for failure. One of them is a lack of clear and concrete Digital Strategy.

Digital Strategy is a prerequisite to Digital Transformation. It comprises two phases:

- Strategy Creation
- Strategy Execution

More comprehensive the digital strategy, more seamless the digital transformation. The problem is that most incumbents commence digital transformation without a digital strategy. And those who start with one, don't have a good framework that can navigate them through the process.

This book contains a complete end-to-end digital strategy framework, providing a step-by-step guidance during the strategy creation and execution phases.

Although anyone can read and derive benefits from this book, it is primarily for executives, strategists, transformation drivers, and managers at incumbent firms.

The success of this book lies in how effectively the readers apply the framework at their workplace. This book is not just about Information.... It's all about *Transformation*!

Keywords

digital; strategy; framework; incumbents; transformation; disruption; creation; execution

Contents

Praise for Digital Strategy Framework

"In an era where digital technologies are reshaping the business landscape, incumbents face the formidable challenge of not only absorbing but also assimilating them effectively into their operations. Amit Prabhu steps in with a timely solution, presenting a pragmatic approach that seamlessly bridges strategy creation and execution through digital technologies. His framework, practically crafted and widely applicable, provides professionals at all levels and across various functions within incumbent organizations with a valuable lens through which to perceive, comprehend, and navigate the multifaceted opportunities and challenges of digital business transformation. A must-read for those seeking to harness the power of digital to drive organizational success."

—Venkat Venkatraman, David J. McGrath Professor, Boston University Questrom School of Business, Author of *The Digital Matrix: New Rules of Business Transformation through Technology*

"This book is a must-read for leaders and decision-makers at business incumbents looking to refine their approach to implementing digital strategies by blending theoretical knowledge with practical insights. Amit Prabhu with his extensive experience and expertise with incumbent companies, shines through in his clear and concise writing style, making complex concepts simplified and accessible to a broader audience. It's an impressive debut from Amit Prabhu, marking him as an author to watch in the business and technology sphere."

—Albert Bengtson, Co-author of *Principles of Intrapreneurial Capital*, ex-Apple

"This book is an invaluable resource for organizations at any stage of their digital transformation. Amit, a seasoned expert, presents a comprehensive framework that serves as a roadmap to develop and execute a successful digital strategy. What sets this book apart is its emphasis on practicality, providing

readers with actionable insights, best practice examples, and valuable lessons learned from real-world case studies."—**Malcolm Azzopardi, Head of VisionLab & Strategic Narratives, Ericsson**

"Through real-life stories and his own experiences, Amit Prabhu underscores how creating a digital strategy is a prerequisite when initiating a digital transformation and highlights strategy execution as a crucial factor for successful implementation through an easy-to-understand framework applicable to all areas and levels of a business. This book is a must-have for CEOs and their executive leadership teams aiming for success in digital transformation." —**Wanda Grimsgaard, Professor, USN School of Business, University of South-Eastern Norway, Author of *Design and Strategy: A Step-by-Step Guide***

"The book provides a thorough examination of the digital transformation process. It provides actionable advice on how to plan and implement a successful digital transformation strategy. Amit backs up theories and concepts with real-world examples. This approach makes the content highly relatable, allowing readers to grasp the practical applications of digital transformation." —**Vinay Dhar, Co-Founder and Head of Digital Business, Consat Orahi**

Introduction

At corporate networking events, I often meet with executives, strategists, and transformation drivers from some of the top incumbent firms across different industries. I normally ask them, "What is the inspiration behind your decision to digitally transform your firm?" Most of them say they decided to transform because their competitors did so. They felt threatened by too many disruptions. They were pressured by their board members to make their company look "digital." Rarely did anyone say they chose to transform because they saw the market shifts, identified the upcoming opportunities, and thought it was the right time to make the move. The decision to transform was more driven by extrinsic factors than intrinsic. It was more reactive than proactive.

Most of the global incumbents have embarked on the digital transformation journey. But only a few have a clear direction of where they are heading and what they are doing. Some of them rush through the transformation too fast. As a result, they miss out on some critical steps. Some of them move too slowly. As a result, they are late to the market than their competitors. As per a recent study by McKinsey, 70 percent of digital transformation projects fail.[1] A large portion of this 70 percent comprises the incumbents. There are several reasons for failure. One of them is a lack of clear and concrete Digital Strategy. It comprises two phases: Strategy Creation and Strategy Execution. More comprehensive the Digital Strategy, more seamless the Digital Transformation.

The Digital Strategy Framework was developed based on my knowledge and a decade of experience in the IT and Telecommunications industry. For more than 10 years, I was an employee at a leading European incumbent, where I got an opportunity to work in different roles such as Sales, Delivery, Strategy, Consulting, Program Management, and Competence Development, across multiple geographies. The longest I worked at was in the role of a Program Manager, where I was primarily involved in driving the Digital Transformation projects globally. I was a member of a few corporate forums where I connected with many professionals who were driving Digital Transformation at their respective firms. It was great to learn from their stories and experiences.

One such story that struck me the most was of Kumar Sundar Das (name changed), a Transformation Strategist at one of the leading incumbent firms in Scandinavia. His firm operated in five major markets: North America, Europe, Latin America, Africa, and Middle East and Asia Pacific. Kumar Sundar was a part of Digital Transformation Hub (DTH) running centrally from the corporate headquarters. The main objective of the DTH was to develop a Digital Transformation program at a global level and govern the execution across different markets. However, there were different independent Digital Transformation projects running in silos across different parts of the organization. The markets were not aligned. There was no common knowledge sharing and learning. There was no central repository to store reusable assets. The DTH quickly realized this problem and decided to streamline the independent projects under the umbrella of "One Digital Transformation." Kumar Sundar fully supported his team's decision, but he strongly felt that DTH overlooked a very important foundational step: Digital Strategy. He immediately brought it up to the Head of DTH and suggested steps to develop one. But he was quickly dismissed saying that the firm already had a corporate strategy and won't need another one. When he had a closer look at the corporate strategy, he observed that it did not echo well with the DTH objectives. Digital Transformation was not explicitly mentioned in the corporate strategy, and there were no champions in the firm advocating it. For Digital Transformation to succeed, there should be only one strategy: the "Digital Strategy," and it should be the corporate strategy. Nonetheless, the "One Digital Transformation" program was kicked off on the wrong foot, without a Digital Strategy. Soon, his firm faced lots of issues aligning its objectives with the markets. There were lots of internal politics and disagreements. The organization lacked a shared vision. Kumar Sundar told me that if he had been the head of DTH, he would have never kicked off such an expensive program at a global scale without a well-defined Digital Strategy. After 10 months, at the end of the first phase of the program, Kumar Sundar resigned.

After hearing his story, I realized that—*Digital Strategy* is a prerequisite to Digital Transformation. Though there are many books written on Digital Transformation, there are only a few books on its precursor—"Digital Strategy." There is no complete end-to-end Digital Strategy Framework existing in market today, providing step-by-step guidance during the creation and execution phases. I decided to address this gap in this book and provide incumbents with an easy-to-implement framework.

I began having open dialogues with my colleagues in different areas of business and various people in my professional network, outside my company, at various incumbent firms to understand their perspectives and pain points. I found out that they too had similar stories like Kumar Sundar's. The main problem was that most incumbents began Digital Transformation without a Digital Strategy. And those who started with one didn't have a good framework that could navigate them throughout the process. They skipped the important steps of Strategy Creation and struggled with Strategy Execution. I interviewed 33 professionals who directly dealt with Digital Transformation in their daily jobs. Combining their feedback with my professional experience and knowledge, I came up with the first draft of Digital Strategy Framework. After several iterations of incremental improvements and validating it with few incumbents in Nordics, I came up with the final "ready-to-use" version.

The Digital Strategy Framework in this book focuses on both Strategy Creation and Execution.

It is primarily for the incumbents who have been operating in one or more industries for a long time. As shown in Figure I.1, it begins with Strategy Creation. The first step in Strategy Creation is Digital Maturity Assessment. It is followed by Industry Analysis, Customer Analysis, Process Analysis, People Analysis, Data Analysis, and IT Tools Analysis.

Digital Maturity Assessment indicates at what level a firm is in the Digital Transformation journey. It is a survey to be completed by different stakeholders such as the executives, department heads, managers, strategists, and transformation drivers. The higher the number of participants, more accurate the response. In *Industry Analysis*, we take a closer look at the single industry or the multiple industries a firm operates in. We do a deep dive on areas such as the main players, competitors, and disruption threats to determine the industry profitability. Based on this analysis, a firm can adapt its positioning in the market. *Customer Analysis* helps you understand in detail who the customers are, what are their needs, how are their needs changing, how are we adding value to our customers,

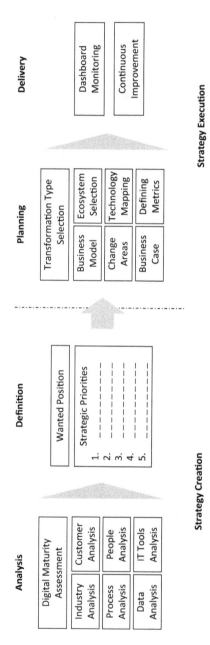

Figure I.1 Digital Strategy Framework

and how are our customers adding value to us. Based on the analysis, one may design a new customer engagement approach. In *Process Analysis*, we list down all the processes in a firm. Then assign a scoring to each process based on an assessment criterion. The processes with a higher score are the ones that can be automated. *People Analysis* helps a firm assess what is the current competence level, what is the desired future competence, and what are the main gaps. Based on the outcome, a firm can decide what actions are to be taken to bridge the competence gaps. *Data Analysis* helps a firm to identify sensitive, private, and confidential data. It addresses the questions: What data flows at customer touchpoints? What data flows across functions? What data flows within functions? Based on this, a firm can decide the necessary steps to protect the data integrity and build a robust data architecture. *IT Tools Analysis* helps to understand which tools add value to the business, which tools can be upgraded, and which tools can be eliminated, based on certain criteria. It can serve as a vital input for a firm to plan and invest in platforms, infrastructures, or cloud strategies.

Based on the outcome of these analyses, we enter the Definition phase, where we define a Digital Strategy, comprising a Wanted Position and Strategic Priorities. A *Wanted Position* is an indication of where a firm wants to be in the next "x" number of months. *Strategic Priorities* explain how a firm can reach its wanted position.

Next comes Strategy Execution. It is divided into Planning and Delivery phases. At the *Planning* phase, we select the Transformation Type, followed by Business Model selection, Ecosystem selection, Identification of Change Areas, Technology Mapping, Business Case, and Defining Metrics. The *Transformation Type* selection includes Core business transformation, Support function transformation, and Industry re-invention transformation.[2] *Business Model* selection involves asking the following questions:

What is the current business model?
Is it sufficient to implement the new digital strategic priorities?
What are the gaps?
How should we mitigate them?
How do we want to conduct our new business?

Which business model should we select?

Next is *Ecosystem* selection. An Ecosystem is defined as a group or cohort with certain business objectives, where people seek and share knowledge and information with one another. A firm must evaluate the best ecosystem it can participate in, where it can add as well as extract significant value. *Identification of Change Areas* is a very important step of Strategy Execution. There are many areas in a firm that need to be transformed. However, priority must be given to those closely aligned with the Strategic Priorities. The next step is *Technology Mapping*. It involves identifying which digital technologies are to be used to transform the identified change areas. The popular digital technologies to select from are AI, Automation, Data Science and Data Analytics, Cloud, Blockchain, IoT, 5G, Gamification, Extended Reality, and Metaverse. The next step is to calculate the *Business Case* for each of the change areas in terms of increase in revenues, reduction in costs, and improvements in customer experience. The last step is *Defining Metrics* for each strategic priority. It is also known as the KPI or Key Performance Indicator. A KPI contains a KPI statement, a target, and the performance indicators.

Next is the *Delivery* phase. It comprises Dashboard Monitoring and Continuous Improvement. *Dashboard Monitoring* involves continuously monitoring the real-time KPI performance via a dashboard. Each employee at different levels in the corporate hierarchy can monitor the performance via a dashboard as per the access permissions and policies defined by the firm. To enable *Continuous Improvement,* one must secure continuous feedback. The Strategy Creation and Execution must be continuous and iterative. One must constantly track the execution as per the defined metrics and seek continuous feedback from the concerned business stakeholders to evaluate the strategic priorities. If some things don't work right, then quick actions need to be taken to change a strategic priority completely.

Strategy Creation and Execution using the above framework involves teamwork. Different people from different cross-functional teams must participate in the development workshops. The framework should be primarily used at the companywide group level. It should be one of the top priorities for the CEO and his/her Executive Leadership team. The

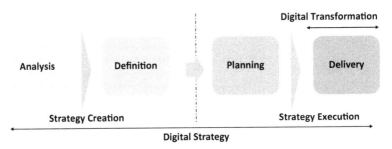

Figure I.2 Relation between Digital Strategy and Digital Transformation

overall group strategic priorities can be broken down into subpriorities for every business unit, which can be further broken down for every team.

Figure I.2 shows how Digital Strategy is a precursor to Digital Transformation. Digital Strategy implies planning, while Digital Transformation implies action or implementation. It begins at the Delivery phase of Strategy Execution.

The book contains six chapters. Chapter 1 deals with the challenges faced by the incumbents. Then, from Chapters 2–4, we discuss the different components of the framework in detail. They contain group activities. Chapter 5 is all about Digital Transformation. In Chapter 6, we discuss about the practical aspects of implementing the Digital Strategy Framework through a fictitious case study. There is an appendix at the end that contains information on Digital Technologies.

Best, I would suggest the readers to read the book sequentially. But if someone has less time at disposal and wants to jump to the practical applications of the framework, then I would suggest reading chapters two, three, four, and six first and the remaining ones later.

The success of this book lies in how effectively the readers apply the framework at their workplace. This book is not just about Information.... It's all about *Transformation*!

CHAPTER 1

Incumbent Challenges

In the digital age, incumbents are constantly facing disruption threats from digital attackers. Incumbents are born in the predigital era and have been in business for many years, in one or more than one industry. They have healthy customer relationships, strong market branding, and the power to change the dynamics of an industry. They are generally mid-to-large sized. Most of them have global operations. There is a peculiar corporate culture, with a systematic organizational hierarchy. Work is mostly done in a more conventional way following set processes, procedures, and patterns. They have the "incumbent's advantage" to exploit new technologies to generate new revenue streams or improve the existing ones.

Digital attackers are the firms that disrupt an incumbent's business. They can be anyone: new digital start-ups or even competitor incumbents. The attacks can happen in one or more than one of the three direct indicators of a company's success: revenues, costs, and customer experience.

In the Telecommunications industry in the 1990s decade, during the 2G GSM era, the main sources of revenue for the telco incumbents were voice and SMS. The highest data speed available was 128 kbps, provided by General Packet Radio Service or GPRS. Yes-128 kbps!—a speed that is hard to imagine today. However, as the need for high-speed data became stronger, technology standards such as 3G UMTS and subsequently 4G LTE appeared on the scene and promised theoretical data speeds up to 100 Mbps. This gave rise to *digital attack on revenues* from new OTT players such as WhatsApp, which leveraged on the network infrastructure provided by these technologies, launched their own services, and started cannibalizing the telco incumbent's main revenue sources. As a result, the telco incumbents had to shift to data as their new mainstream revenue source.

An example of *digital attack on costs* is the disruption caused in the real estate construction market by the 3D printing construction companies.

In 2021, Tvasta, an Indian start-up built the nation's first 3D-printed house[1] on the campus of the Indian Institute of Technology (IIT), Madras. Proprietary software developed by Tvasta created digital blueprints of different parts of the home. These parts were constructed at an offsite location by 3D printers, who deposited different layers of concrete in a specific way as per the commands given by the software program. They were transported to IIT to be assembled on-site. Then, the final works such as interiors, paintings, and furnishings were completed. The whole process took only 21 days. A 3D-printed two-bedroom home can cost somewhere between $5000 and $12,000 to construct, way cheaper than the homes built by the incumbent construction companies, due to significant reductions in labor, transportation, and logistics costs.

Sephora, a French multinational retailer of personal care and beauty products, opened its first store in New York City in 1998. It provided a different experience to its customers by encouraging them to try and test the products in retail stores before purchasing. Birchbox, a company founded in 2010 in New York City, disrupted this setup by launching a *digital attack on customer experience*. It allowed customers to test products in more comfortable and relaxed environments such as homes, spas, and beauty parlors, besides brick-and-mortar stores. Each month, for a basic subscription service of $10,[2] the customer would receive a box of four to five selected samples of makeup, or other beauty-related products such as skincare items, perfumes, and organic-based products.[3] If users liked the sample, they could purchase the full-sized products online from Birchbox's website. The customer preferences were better understood through a "beauty profile" survey.[4] Also, Birchbox offered editorial content on how to best use the samples, a loyalty program including points for purchases, referrals, and surveys, to be redeemed toward the purchase of full-sized products, and a tracker that helped the manufacturers of beauty products measure the return on marketing investments by tracking which subscribers received samples and how much of the full-priced product was purchased later by them from Birchbox's website.[5] This contrasted with the traditional marketing approach where free product samples were usually given away initially to build a customer base and where the success conversation rate with loyal and paying customers was difficult to determine.[6]

Incumbents must transform their businesses digitally to stay competitive and relevant in the market. Because if they don't, their survival is under jeopardy. I would like to provide examples of two incumbents: Burberry (clothing) and MIT/Harvard (education), who successfully transformed themselves and two incumbents: Kodak (photography) and Blockbuster (video rentals), who had to shut down due to their inability to transform at the right time.

Burberry, a 150-year-old British luxury fashion brand, saw the upcoming shifts in the customer needs and kicked-off several digital initiatives. It built a solid transformation foundation through business wide investments in SAP technology. It started to allocate more advertising budget to digital marketing, slowly moving away from traditional media. In 2009, it started engaging with customers over social media such as Facebook, Twitter, and YouTube and created its own social networking site called artofthetrench.com, where followers from all over the world submitted a picture of themselves wearing the trademark Burberry clothes. To garner the attention of millennials, Burberry partnered with Google to create "Burberry kisses," a social media campaign allowing users to send virtual kisses in Burberry lipstick colors via a camera or touchscreen device. The journey of each kiss was tracked using Google Earth and Street View and then displayed to their loved ones. It attracted visitors from 200 countries, thus creating a novel way to attract new customers to the brand. In 2010, it launched Burberry Acoustic, which featured British bands and artists performing acoustic tracks wearing items from the latest Burberry collections. It created Burberry chat, an internal messaging platform based on Salesforce's Chatter, which served as a link between sales associates, head office, and external partners in real time. Burberry also focused on offering personalized experiences to its customers by enabling them to design customized trench coats, selecting cut, fabric, and color, and adding accents such as bronze-studded sleeves or leather cuff straps through Burberry Bespoke. In 2012, it launched Burberry World, the biggest and most technically advanced store. Clothing was embedded with RFID chips, which could be read by instore mirrors. When a customer entered a changing room with a jacket, for instance, the mirrors were converted into screens showcasing how that garment was worn on the catwalk, providing details of how it was made, or suggesting accessories that would complement the item. Burberry invested in Data Analytics to better understand customer's shopping behavior. It captured customer data in about 85 percent of transactions and had nine million customers in its database, which was used to improve customer experience, store productivity, and helped management make informed decisions.[7] Thus, Burberry was able to secure new revenue streams through digital transformation.

Early 2010 saw disruptions in the education industry with digital technologies enabling the rise of new alternative online learning solutions called Massive Open Online Courses (MOOCs). With free education content available from Khan Academy and YouTube, the incumbent educational institutions were compelled to find digital solutions that offered new value propositions to their customers. To remain competitive in the market, the education incumbents MIT and Harvard invested $30 million[8] each into a new venture called "edX," which allowed professors from leading universities across the globe to offer courses over the online platform. One need not be an MIT or Harvard student to sign up for these courses. Practically anyone could sign up for certification courses from these top-ranked institutions for a minimal fee, or even free of cost. Anant Agarwal, the founder of edX and a professor at MIT explained, "For us, it is not about MOOCs. We are trying to reimagine campus education from the ground up—new ways of learning that are more enriching, more engaging, more efficient, and that produce better outcomes."[9] As a result, edX courses were primarily targeted at supplementing, rather than replacing classroom teaching.[10]

For almost a century, Kodak was a leader in the photography industry owning lots of innovations. It was the first company to take photography out of the studio and make it accessible to common people. Kodak followed a razor-and-blade business model, where it sold the Kodak camera at a lower price and made huge profits on the Kodak camera film. The customers would take photos using the Kodak camera and send the film to the Kodak factory, where it was developed and printed. In 1980, there was a transformation in the photography industry and things started shifting toward digital. Digital cameras started to appear on the horizon. Kodak, though being the inventor of digital camera, was blind to this trend and continued with its profitable camera and film business with a dominant market share of 85 percent in analog cameras and 90 percent in film.[11] It received strong competition from Fuji, a Japanese company, which took a major chunk of customers away from Kodak, by offering a film 20 percent cheaper than Kodak's. Instead of focusing on the new digital market, Kodak became busy competing with Fuji. From 2000 to 2009, the digital camera sales began to increase, while the analog camera sales started to decline. Kodak released some digital products, but it was too late to secure a good positioning in the market. Sales kept on falling and finally in 2012 Kodak filed for bankruptcy.[12]

Before Netflix or Amazon Prime dominated the video streaming market, it was the era of Blockbuster, the largest video rental store with 9000 locations around the world and a customer base of 50 million. Customers had to visit a Blockbuster store to rent their favorite movies on VHS tapes or DVDs. One of the main sources of revenue for Blockbuster was the late fees the customers had to pay if they did not return the movie rental on time. It amounted to $800 million in 2000, which was 16 percent of Blockbuster's revenue.[13] Customers didn't like paying the late fees, including Reed Hastings, the founder of Netflix. In fact, Hastings started Netflix because he was annoyed with the $40 late fee Blockbuster charged him on the return of the Apollo 13 movie. In 1997, Netflix was founded. Customers liked Netflix, as they no longer had to go to the physical store. They simply had to place an online order for their favorite movie or video game, and it would show up in the mailbox a few days later. Blockbuster, who was initially skeptical about the process of renting DVDs online, later launched a similar service called Blockbuster Online in 2004. But it took six years to do so. Blockbuster knew that the next shift would be from physical renting to online streaming of videos, but it was unable to move away from its mainstream and slow-declining movie rental business. Meanwhile, Netflix was able to digitally transform itself to streaming, disrupting its own DVD rental business. With one billion dollars in debt, finally in 2010, Blockbuster filed for bankruptcy. Blockbuster also had the opportunity to buy Netflix for $50 million in 2000.[14] But it declined the deal. The price was too high for them. Some business pundits call it the "biggest miss" of the century.

In his book: The Digital Matrix, Professor Venkat from the Questrom School of Business at Boston University explains the idea of digital transformation landscape comprising digital giants or front-runners, entrepreneurs, and incumbents. The digital front-runners are Amazon, Google, Microsoft, Facebook, and Apple. They either have a strong impact across multiple industries or have the potential to make one in the near future. The entrepreneurs are born digital and generally come up with unique industry-specific solutions. And the incumbents dominate a specific industry for a long time.

In the media industry, the front-runners are Google with YouTube, Amazon with Amazon Prime, Facebook with Facebook Live, Microsoft with Microsoft TV, and Apple with Apple TV. The entrepreneurs are Netflix, Hulu, HBO max, Paramount+, and so on. The incumbents are Disney, Time Warner, BBC, NBC, AT&T, Sky, and so on.

In the education industry, the front-runners are Google with Google Education, Amazon with Amazon Academy, Facebook with Meta for Education, Microsoft with Microsoft Education, and Apple with Apple Education. The entrepreneurs are Udemy, Coursera, edX, Khan Academy, Udacity, and so on. The incumbents are Harvard, Stanford, MIT, Oxford, and so on.

In the automotive industry, the front-runners are Google with Android Auto and Waymo, Amazon with Amazon vehicles, Facebook with marketplace that also connects buyers with sellers of auto spare parts and accessories, Microsoft with its Automotive solutions, and Apple with Apple iCar. The entrepreneurs are Tesla, Oxbotica, Getaround, and so on. The incumbents are Hyundai, Toyota, Ford, Daimler, Volkswagen, and so on.

Among the different players in the digital landscape, the incumbents are the most vulnerable and are constantly facing disruption threats from new entrepreneurs, front-runners, or their competitor incumbents. They need to constantly evolve on the digital transformation journey. But despite having the best possible capabilities to drive change, most incumbents over the past decade have struggled to go digital. The key reasons are lack of Leadership, lack of Technological Competence, lack of Learning Culture, and lack of Digital Strategy.

Lack of Leadership

Last year, I was coaching one of my clients on Digital Leadership. I asked her to make a list of things that needed to change in her organization and a list of actions she should take to make them happen. Then I made her commit to me which I call the "coaching contract" to ensure that she would drive these changes. After pausing for a while, she spoke with a concern,

> All that we agree seems fine to me. I would take the necessary actions. But the bottleneck lies with my top management. They have their own priorities to focus and would take lots of time to approve my new ideas.

No matter how good your ideas are, they will fail if there is no timely and adequate support from the leadership. A good digital leader should empower his or her team to take ownership of tasks and make quick decisions. When a leader keeps all decision-making power to himself/herself and does not delegate enough, it creates lots of delays and longer lead times in getting things done.

In 2016, I moved to Scandinavia to work at my company's headquarters. The company was in the middle of a reorganization. Things were very uncertain and chaotic. Most of the major decisions were on hold. The manager who had initially hired me for the position had left the company. There was no one to onboard me into the new team and help me settle down. I was working under an acting manager, who gave me some assignments to begin with. Then, after three months, I had a new manager. I scheduled a meeting with him to discuss some of the issues I had with the assignment I was working on. We met and discussed for 45 minutes. While I was leaving the meeting room, he smiled gently and told me next time I meet him, I should come up with some solution options too, and not just problem statements. By doing so, our meetings would be shorter and very effective. He empowered me to make decisions. That's the mark of a leader. I thanked him for his feedback and appreciated him for the great leadership example he was trying to set forth for the team in the middle of a crisis.

Lack of Technological Competence

Most incumbents find it difficult to find people with the right digital skills as demanded by the new digital technologies. As per the report by the World Economic Forum, there is a global shortage of digital skills, which could mean 85 million jobs would remain unfilled by 2030.[15] Businesses in all sectors need to have a long-term strategy for developing them. If the right competence cannot be acquired externally, it is best to build it internally through upskilling and reskilling programs.

AT&T, the U.S. telecommunications giant realized that its legacy businesses were soon getting obsolete, with the industry moving from cables and hardware to new digital technologies such as Internet, Cloud, and Software-defined networks (SDN). To sustain in the market, it needed people with Cloud, Data Science, and AI skills. Instead of laying off people, AT&T decided to rapidly retrain its workforce of 280,000 employees through a program called Workforce 2020. The program consolidated 250 job roles into 80, to simplify and standardize role structures to add more flexibility and fluidity to the jobs. Performance metrics were simplified to focus more directly on how individuals contributed to business strategies and targets. Performance expectations from the managers and employees were raised. Compensation plans were redesigned to de-emphasize seniority. New tools for career development were provided: a career profile tool for assessing competencies, business experience, and credentials, a career intelligence tool for making informed decisions by analyzing hiring trends within the company for profiles of different jobs, and a job simulation tool presenting realistic job-related situations and rating how people respond to them to assess their suitability for various jobs. Online individual training courses, online nanodegrees, and online master degrees in partnership with Udacity and Georgia Tech were introduced. Employees were expected to adopt a "lattice corporate thinking," where each one would actively own one's career development and explore both lateral and diagonal career moves. Randall Stephenson, the ex-CEO of AT&T told the New York Times, "The company has to look forward and transform; if it doesn't succeed at retraining and reinvention, mark my words, in three years, we will be managing decline."[16]

Lack of Learning Culture

Another reason why incumbents struggle to go digital is a lack of learning culture in the organization. There is an internal resistance to change. People normally like to do what they have been doing for a long and feel insecure when asked to change. New digital technologies open new digital skills and competencies. And, to ensure that such skillsets are developed, an organization must give up its old culture and embrace a new culture of learning. As per the 70:20:10 rule, 70 percent of the learning happens on the job, 20 percent through collaborations, and 10 percent through classroom and web-based training courses.[17] Learning is something that needs to be owned by an individual. If employees don't receive proper or no training on new technologies, it might lead to their dissatisfaction and eventually quitting.

Digiculum, a learning ecosystem orchestration firm, based out of Stockholm, Sweden, in its blog,[18] explains how learning in an organization should be able to create better user experiences:

a. Learning should be *personalized*. It should be distinct and unique for each user based on its job requirements. Suggestions and recommendations for new courses should be offered based on the courses previously enrolled in or completed.

b. Learning should be *easy*. It should be well-structured and easy to access. Users must be able to reach the desired content in a few clicks.

c. Learning should be *collaborative*. There should be a central repository to store all the learning and users must be able to share knowledge assets easily across different teams and functions.

d. Learning should be *insightful*. Learning should be data driven based on advanced analytics and tools. Individual users should be able to monitor their real-time progress on a dashboard. Organizations should be able to track learning performance and make informed decisions based on learning behaviors, patterns, and insights.

e. Learning should be *progressive*. Users should be offered clear upskilling or reskilling learning plans or pathways leading to one's individual development and career growth.

f. Learning should be *seamless*. The end-to-end process from enrolling to final completion, in either a web-based or instructor-driven course, should be smooth and continuous.

g. Learning should be *inspiring*. Organizations should cultivate a culture of learning and innovations where users are inspired to learn and share more.

Lack of Strategy

A company where employees are aware of its corporate strategy is more likely to perform better than the one where employees are not. When employees are unclear, different teams might end up having different objectives. The technical team might want to solve technical problems only without worrying much about the business. The marketing team might want to generate leads, regardless of their conversion to sales. The sales team might want to focus on closing deals without aligning much with the delivery team. In such a situation where there is no shared vision, it might be hard to seek commitment from different teams to make the digital transformation successful.

General Electric Digital, better known as GE Digital, lacked a shared vision, which eventually led to its failure. It was formed in 2015 as a separate business unit with the objective of bringing all the digital capabilities from across the company into one organization. After Jack Welch's tenure as a CEO was over in 2001, Jeffery Immelt stepped in. He was an 18-year GE veteran, who had held leadership positions in GE's Plastics, Appliances, and Healthcare business. Immelt had a digital vision to transform GE into a tech company, more than just an industrial conglomerate. The following six key strategic priorities were developed:

1. Divest nonindustrial and slow-growth businesses.
2. Focus on high-tech and manufacturing-based products and services.
3. Invest in technology-driven innovation, by increasing spend on R&D and focusing on cleantech and energy-efficient products, Internet of Things (IoT), and additive manufacturing.
4. Expand more into developed and emerging markets outside the United States.

5. Agile and decentralized organization structure.
6. Move away from commoditized hardware to high-margin business models enabled by smart and connected products.

Immelt could foresee that data would be a very important commodity in the future, more important than the industrial hardware or systems generating it. So, companies who figure out how to monetize from data would have better control over the industrial companies. GE had a huge customer base using GE's industrial hardware and equipment. Immelt wanted to create new revenue streams and value from the data generated by these systems. IT giants such as IBM, Microsoft, and SAP already had started to approach GE's customers with propositions on how to make the best use of data generated by GE systems.

Immelt and his team of strategists were amazed by the vast industrial opportunities the IoT could offer. Traditional devices, if IoT-enabled could report back to the manufacturer: how well they were functioning, whether they needed further improvements, whether they needed servicing, how they were used by the customers, and even what customers were saying about them. He wanted to build an Industrial IoT platform to secure a dominant position and the first-mover advantage in the ecosystem. He knew that if a third-party software firm developed a winner-take-all platform that captured the analytics layer, GE could be forced to join the platform and cede a great deal of the value of its equipment, including its maintenance services, to the owner of the platform. In other words, a tech company could achieve a dominant position in the industrial IoT ecosystem, like the one Microsoft held in the desktop PC ecosystem.

There was already strong competition from IBM with its Watson, Philips with its HealthSuite digital platform, Toshiba with its IoT architecture called SPINEX, Google with its Things platform of IoT products and services, Microsoft with its Azure IoT capabilities, Cisco with its IoT and analytical software offerings, Honeywell with its cloud-enabled software service IoT, Amazon with its IoT cloud platform, and Siemens with its MindSphere 3.0, a cloud-based open IoT operating system.

To stay relevant and competitive, GE developed an IoT platform named Predix, that provided applications like preventive maintenance, process variance reduction, control system optimization, and manufacturing productivity in various industries such as aviation, pharmaceuticals, power, mining, manufacturing, and oil and gas. GE started engagements with customers and partners to use the Predix platform for their industrial activities, positioning itself as an industry expert, unlike its competition. GE also began to offer pilots to existing clients. However, the internal departments within GE had diverse views and opinions on how Predix should be offered to its existing clients.

GE Digital had three Go-to-market options on how to sell the Predix to customers. First, a "bundled" option. It involved bundling Predix's data analytics along with hardware and maintenance service sales. Second, an "unbundled" option. It involved creating a new consulting unit for Predix data analytics solutions and selling separately from hardware and services. Third, an "outcome-based" option, where the customer pays only if the business achieves the necessary outcomes. This was radically different from its traditional approach of selling hardware, where the implementation risk would be transferred to GE Digital and the customers would need to pay a risk premium. GE Digital chose the third option.

The main challenge with the outcome-based option was that GE Digital needed to understand the client business in detail to agree on reliable metrics that measured outcomes. This required the sales team, who were experts in selling traditional hardware, to adopt a new way of selling. Also, the customers needed to have enough trust in Predix, to allow the GE sales team to dive deeper into its business details and open access to its internal data.

Predix received a pushback from GE's internal IT team. To develop some capabilities, it needed support from them. However, the IT was too busy with supporting the existing legacy businesses and had less bandwidth to support Predix. To counter that, Predix hired external technical people, who struggled to come on the same page with GE's IT. There were some software glitches in Predix, and it lacked some capabilities that GE's legacy platforms had, which added more strain to the already existing weak relationship between GE IT and GE Digital. Its strategy to host Predix on public cloud providers such as Amazon Web Services and Microsoft Azure, added more fuel to the fire.

Most GE customers were not digitally savvy. They didn't know how to make the best use of data collected by Predix. Beth Comstock, GE's Chief Marketing Officer explained: "We're trying to sell them something they don't know they need." Also, it was bad timing for Predix as other GE businesses such as GE Power, GE Capital were not doing well and there were some accounting problems within the company on which the U.S. Securities and Exchange Commission (SEC) had raised concerns. There were layoffs in the company and some of its executives, who once believed strongly in GE Digital's vision left.[19]

So, what went wrong at GE? Some argue that the strategy was flawed. Some blame the bad timing. Some feel that it didn't persist enough and gave up too soon. Some think it was too focused on developing Predix without a solid rollout plan.

I would say there was no FRAMEWORK.

Summary

- Digital attackers launch three types of disruption attacks on the incumbents: attack on revenue, attack on costs, and attack on customer experience.
- Incumbents must transform digitally to survive the competition and stay relevant in the market.
- Digital landscape comprises front-runners, entrepreneurs, and incumbents.
- The main reasons why incumbents fail to transform digitally are lack of Leadership, lack of Technological Competence, lack of Learning Culture, and lack of Digital Strategy.
- Incumbents have the advantage of exploiting digital transformation using a Digital Strategy Framework explained in this book.

CHAPTER 2

Digital Strategy Creation

The Digital Strategy Framework shown in Figure 2.1 contains two phases:

- Strategy Creation
- Strategy Execution

Strategy Creation contains two phases:

- Analysis
- Definition

Digital Maturity Assessment

It is the first step in the Analysis phase. *Digital Maturity Assessment* is an end-to-end analysis that shows at what level your firm is in the digital transformation journey. The Digital Maturity of an organization is modeled in two dimensions:

- New Business Adoption
- Digital Technology Adoption

New Business Adoption is defined as the ability of an organization to adopt best practices and new ways of working to improve Customer Engagement, Internal Operations, and Corporate Culture. *Digital Technology Adoption* is the ability of an organization to adopt new digital technologies to drive business transformation.

Based on the model, we can assess the digital maturity of an organization at the following five levels: Level 1, Level 2, Level 3, Level 4, and Level 5 as shown in Figure 2.2.

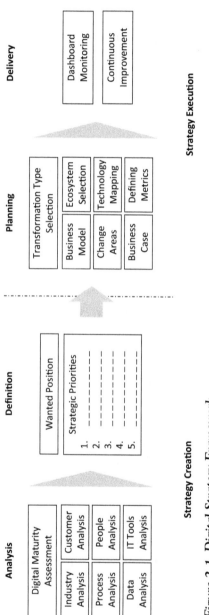

Figure 2.1 Digital Strategy Framework

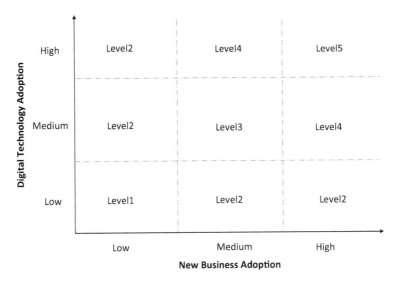

Figure 2.2 Digital Maturity Assessment Levels

At *Level 1,* both New Business Adoption and Digital Technology Adoption are low. You don't have a clear understanding of your customer's changing needs. The internal processes are manual, time-consuming, and follow the same old repetitive procedures. Corporate culture is very rigid and inflexible. People lack new digital skills, and there is an unwillingness to learn, grow, and innovate. You lack a clear Digital Strategy.

Level 2 corresponds to low New Business Adoption and medium or high Digital Technology Adoption, or medium or high New Business Adoption and low Digital Technology Adoption. You have somewhat understanding of changing customer needs but you have no strategy or plan on how to fulfill them. Very few internal processes are automated and most of them still need human intervention. Corporate culture has the potential to change but no concrete actions are taken to get rid of old beliefs and practices. People have moderate digital skills but still, there is an unwillingness to learn, grow, and innovate. You have somewhat clarity on what changes to make but are unclear about how to drive them.

At *Level 3,* both New Business Adoption and Digital Technology Adoption are medium. You understand your customer needs but are unable to drive Digital Transformation discussions or engagements with them. Your internal operations are streamlined with a good mix of both manual and automated processes. You have a good strategy and plan in place to change your corporate culture but haven't really embarked on the journey yet. You have good technical learning and development plans, and the development of digital competence is ongoing. You have good clarity on the overall strategy and have taken a few initial steps to execute it.

Level 4 corresponds to high New Business Adoption and medium Digital Technology Adoption or medium New Business Adoption and high Digital Technology Adoption. You have a good understanding of your customer needs and can drive a meaningful discussion on Digital Transformation with them. Most of your internal operations are automated. Your corporate culture is flexible, and you are in the process of transforming it. The digital competence is high, and people take ownership of their personal learning and development. You have a concrete strategy in place and have good management and control over its execution.

At *Level 5*, both New Business Adoption and Digital Technology Adoption are high. You have strong relationships with your customers and empathize with their needs. You not only can engage in valuable discussions but also consult and educate them on best digital practices and procedures and how to take advantage of new digital opportunities. Your internal operations are fully automated, efficient, and effective. You have a great corporate culture of learning and innovation. The digital competence of your people is very high, and there is lots of knowledge sharing and collaboration among the teams. You have a concrete and well-defined digital strategy and exemplify superior strategy execution.

Group Activity

1. Distribute the assessment questionnaire to all the key stakeholders in your organization. It contains a total of 65 questions: 35 for New Business Adoption and 30 for Digital Technology Adoption. New Business Adoption is divided into the following domains: Customer Engagement, Internal Operations, and Corporate Culture. Digital Technology Adoption is divided into Data, IT tools, Apps, and Technical Competence.

2. To each statement in the assessment, assign a score between 1 and 6, depending on the extent to which you agree or disagree:
   1. Strongly Disagree
   2. Disagree
   3. Somewhat Disagree
   4. Somewhat Agree
   5. Agree
   6. Strongly Agree
3. For New Business Adoption, calculate the average score for Customer Engagement, Internal Operations, and Corporate Culture. Similarly, for Digital Technology Adoption, calculate the average score for Data, IT tools, Apps, and Technical Competence.
4. Add the average scores for New Business Adoption to arrive at a final score. Compare the final score with the following legend:
   between 3 and 8: Low
   between 9 and 15: Medium
   between 16 and 18: High
5. Add the average scores for Digital Technology Adoption to arrive at a final score. Compare the final score with the following legend:
   between 4 and 10: Low
   between 11 and 19: Medium
   between 20 and 24: High
6. Use the grid in Figure 2.2 to determine the maturity level.

Assessment Questionnaire

	New Business Adoption	Your Score
	Customer Engagement	
1	We clearly understand our customer's business needs	
2	We translate customer needs into solutions	
3	We constantly put into perspective how work relates to customer success	
4	We seek continuous feedback from customers	
5	We constantly innovate new ways of engaging with customer	
6	Our sales team is competent with new digital skills	
7	Customer data is accessible to us in real-time	

(Continues)

(Continued)

	New Business Adoption	Your Score
8	Our customer processes are automated	
9	We receive continuous data on our product/service performance	
10	We have a culture of customer first	
11	Our customers trust us as reliable partners	
12	We offer better experience to our customers	
13	We have better insights on our customers	
14	We have efficient systems to track customer behavior	
a)	Average Score	
	Internal Operations	
15	Our internal business processes are automated	
16	We monitor our internal operational processes in real-time	
17	We make decisions based on data analytics	
18	We use dashboards to monitor the operational KPIs	
19	Our supplier processes are automated	
20	We can monitor our supplier data in real-time	
21	We achieve considerable cost savings through our digitalized operations	
22	We have integrated financial data and systems	
23	We have digitalized our HR processes	
24	We manage our inventories in real-time	
b)	Average Score	
	Corporate Culture	
25	People have desire to learn new digital skills	
26	People are willing to invest time and effort in learning	
27	We have an effective individual learning system	
28	We innovate continuously	
29	We often share knowledge and re-use information	
30	Our leaders exemplify a culture of learning and innovation	
31	We offer psychological safety to our employees	
32	We have a strong feedback system	
33	We have a startup culture	
34	We orchestrate ecosystems at our workplace	
35	We have a clear digital transformation strategy	
c)	Average Score	
	Final Score: a + b + c	

	Digital Technology Adoption	Your Score
	Data	
1	Our data is available in real-time	
2	Our data is easily accessible	
3	Our data flows seamlessly between the systems	
4	We derive useful insights from our data	
5	We have efficient data aggregation and curation methods	
6	We capture data at various touch points across our customer journey	
7	We make data-driven business decisions	
8	We have rigid data security and integrity measures	
a)	Average Score	
	IT Tools	
9	We understand the business criticality of the tools	
10	We continuously monitor our tool usage	
11	We continuously upgrade our tools	
12	We know the operational costs of all our tools	
13	Our tools offer data and information security	
14	Our tools are customizable	
15	Our tools are reusable	
16	Our tools integrate well with other tools in our IT environment	
17	We have a good control over redundant tools	
18	We use virtual assistants/chatbots for IT support	
b)	Average Score	
	Apps	
19	We have migrated most of the applications to cloud	
20	We have a good cloud migration strategy	
21	We innovate in cloud	
c)	Average Score	
	Technical Competence	
22	We have strong AI/ML competence	
23	We have strong Automation competence	
24	We have strong IoT competence	
25	We have strong Data Science competence	
26	We have strong Cloud competence	
27	We have strong Digital Marketing competence	

(Continues)

(*Continued*)

	Digital Technology Adoption	Your Score
28	We have strong Coding skills	
29	We have strong Platform Engineering skills	
30	We have strong IT infrastructure management skills	
d)	Average Score	
	Final Score: a + b + c + d	

Industry Analysis

Industry Analysis determines if your current industry is profitable enough to sustain your business in the rapidly evolving digital age. As per Porter's five forces framework, the major forces in any industry that impact profitability are:

- Threat of New Entrants
- Bargaining Power of Suppliers
- Bargaining Power of Buyers
- Availability of Substitutes
- Rivalry among Competitors[1]

If a firm's industry profitability is low, it must carefully evaluate all the existing forces and develop a strategy to improve it. These forces keep on changing constantly. Hence it is important to do Industry Analysis whenever a firm wants to develop a new digital strategy or revise its existing one. These forces might change for a given industry across different markets and geographies. For example, the profitability of the healthcare industry in the United States might be different from the one in India.

When the *Threat of New Entrants* is high, the profitability of incumbents operating in a given industry is low. It is dependent on the following seven factors:

- Capital requirements at entry
- Switching costs
- Power of incumbents

- Limitations of distribution channel
- Ease of doing business
- Exit costs
- Industry growth

The new entrants could be entrepreneurs, incumbents, or front-runners. The following table shows the relationship of these factors with the threat of new entrants:

Factors	Threat of New Entrants	Examples
Capital requirements at entry	Inversely Proportional	Capital-intensive industries are airlines, automotive, mining, oil and gas, and manufacturing[2]
Switching costs	Inversely Proportional	A company with huge investments in software from a given supplier might be reluctant to switch to a new one as the costs of switching would be high
Power of incumbents	Inversely Proportional	In industries such as life sciences, alcoholic beverages, diversified chemicals,[3] incumbents have high power
Limitations of distribution channel	Inversely Proportional	Film industry where only a few film makers can take the movie to cinema houses due to limited distribution channels
Ease of doing business	Directly Proportional	The ease of doing business ranking for Sweden (81.27) is higher than China (65.29), making it difficult for new entrants to enter the Chinese market than the Swedish[4]
Exit Costs	Inversely Proportional	Specialized manufacturing is an example of an industry with high exit costs[5]
Industry Growth	Directly Proportional	In Q3 2022, mining and quarrying was the industry with the slowest growth rate[6]

The Power of incumbents depends on the following five factors:

- Fixed costs per unit
- Perceived product value based on networking effects

- Number of products/services sold to a single customer
- Control over product/service pricing
- Good track record of mitigating threats from disrupters

Imagine there is a well-established incumbent "I" and a new entrant "E" in an industry. Both incur the same fixed costs. However, for "I" the quantity of supply is larger than "E," which reduces the cost per unit. This is known as *Economies of Scale.* "I" can control the end price of the product/service which might be difficult for "E" to compete. This places "I" in a higher power position. For I, more people are buying a similar product than E. The perceived value of the product for I increases due to a phenomenon known as the "networking effect," putting I in a higher power position. An example of the networking effect is Amazon. The potential value to a customer from buying or selling on Amazon depends on the number of other buyers and sellers who use it. More the buyers and sellers more will be the product value. If "I" is selling more products/services to a customer "C" than "E," then it has good control over pricing and better chances of selling more in the future to "C" than "E." This places "I" in a higher power position. If "I" has a good track record of mitigating threats from disruptors, it has a higher power position than "E."

Limitations of distribution channels are inversely proportional to the threat of new entrants. Imagine there are only three distributors D1, D2, and D3, and "I" has an exclusive contract with all three of them, it would be difficult for "E" to find a foot in the distribution channel.

When the Bargaining Power of Suppliers is high, they can better control the prices, which reduces the profitability of incumbents operating in a given industry. The affecting factors are:

- Supplier dominance
- Switching costs
- Differentiated products
- Few or no substitute products
- Multiple industry supply

The following table shows the relationship of these factors with the bargaining power of suppliers:

Factors	Bargaining Power of Suppliers	Examples
Supplier Dominance	Directly Proportional	In the PC manufacturing industry, companies such as Microsoft with its Windows operating system and Intel with its chipsets, have a strong supplier dominance and better control over pricing
Switching Costs	Directly Proportional	In the telecommunications industry, the costs of switching from one Network Equipment Provider (NEP) to another is higher
Differentiated Products	Directly Proportional	ChatGPT, launched in November 2022 by OpenAI, is an example of a highly differentiated product with a unique positioning
Few or no substitute products	Inversely Proportional	Giffen goods[7] such as wheat, potatoes, rice, salt have almost no substitutes
Multiple industry supply	Directly Proportional	Suppliers in the aviation industry, who supply products exclusively to aircraft manufacturers, have less bargaining power

When the Bargaining Power of Buyers is high, the profitability for the incumbents in a given industry is low. The affecting factors are:

- Customer dominance
- Switching costs
- Undifferentiated products or services

The following table shows the relationship of these factors with the bargaining power of buyers.

Factors	Bargaining Power of Buyers	Examples
Customer dominance	Directly Proportional	Boeing and Airbus being the only two large aircraft manufacturers have better dominance over their suppliers, thus resulting in higher bargaining power

(Continues)

(*Continued*)

Factors	Bargaining Power of Buyers	Examples
Switching costs	Inversely Proportional	In the beverage industry, the costs of switching from Pepsi to Coca-Cola are low, providing more power to the buyers
Undifferentiated products or services	Directly Proportional	For example, in the airline industry, the customers have a higher bargaining power as the services offered by different airlines are almost the same

When the Availability of Substitutes is high, the profitability of the incumbents in a given industry is low. Examples of substitutes are videoconferencing for business air travel, public transport for personal vehicles, online retailers for brick-and-mortar stores, home cooking for restaurants, and book reading for YouTube videos. The availability of substitutes depends on the ease of access. For example, a family might prefer cooking at home to eating at a restaurant on a cold and rainy evening. The substitute of eating at a restaurant is available but not easily accessible due to bad weather.

When there are two or more incumbents in a given industry, they compete over price, which reduces the profitability of the industry. The factors that impact the competition are:

- Commoditization of products
- Switching costs
- Industry growth
- Exit barriers

The following table shows the relationship of these factors with the rivalry among competitors.

Factors	Rivalry among Competitors	Examples
Commoditization of products	Directly Proportional	The rivalry between Pepsi and Coke
Switching costs	Inversely Proportional	Switching costs from one telco operator to another is low, resulting in higher rivalry

Factors	Rivalry among Competitors	Examples
Industry Growth	Inversely Proportional	In Q3 2022, mining and quarrying was the industry with the slowest growth rate[8]
Exit Barriers	Directly Proportional	Specialized manufacturing

If the products are almost similar and not differentiated, they get commoditized, and a price war commences between the competitor incumbents. When the costs of switching from one incumbent to another are low, the rivalry among the competition is intense. When the industry growth is slow, the competition is high as the incumbents fight to steal the market share from one another. When the cost of exiting an industry is high, the competition is high, as competitors have no choice but to stay in the game and compete with one another.

Let us try to understand the profitability of the Media, Education, and Automotive industries. For the Media industry, we consider both the traditional and the digital media and combine all the different sectors such as TV, motion pictures, social media, books, and Internet together.

- The Threat of New Entrants is high as there are low-cost barriers to entry due to rapid rise of Internet and digital technologies. Anyone can create content on free platforms such as YouTube and build a base of thousands of subscribers.
- The Bargaining Power of Suppliers is high since there are many differentiated and unique contents available. For example, J.K Rowling, the author of the famous Harry Potter series, had a strong bargaining power when she licensed her unique content to Warner Bros. for movie production.
- The Bargaining Power of Buyers is high since there are plenty of options available to switch from one content to another, as the cost of switching is very low. If a customer is not satisfied with Amazon Prime, he or she can switch to Netflix very easily.
- The Availability of Substitutes is high. For example, reading a book could be a good substitute for watching a movie on Netflix.

- The Rivalry among Competitors is high. For example, there is an intense competition between big production houses such as Warner Bros., Paramount Pictures Corporation, The Walt Disney Studios, Fox Entertainment Group, and so on, who constantly rival out each other to produce the best content. Taking into consideration all the forces, we can understand that the profitability of Media industry is Low.

Media Industry	Overall profitability is Low
Threat of New Entrants	High
Bargaining Power of Suppliers	High
Bargaining Power of Buyers	High
Availability of Substitutes	High
Rivalry among Competitors	High

In the Education industry,

- The Threat of New Entrants is high as it is not very expensive to create new content and enter the market.
- The Bargaining Power of Suppliers is high. Examples of suppliers in the education industry are teachers, professors, and educational content creators. More differentiated and unique the content, more the bargaining power of suppliers. For example, professors at top universities such as MIT and Harvard have lots of credibility and are valuable assets to the universities that contribute toward its ranking.
- The Bargaining Power of Buyers is high. There are plenty of educational sources available and the cost of switching from one source to another is not very high.
- The Threat of Substitutes is high. The threat for paid education is free education available on online platforms such as YouTube or Udemy. However, the quality of free education may not be the same as the paid one. Alan Garber, the provost of Harvard quoted, "Long run, I see the online courses or online components becoming pervasive. Instructors in a

seminar or small course might obtain modular materials from multiple sources and assemble them in order to put together an entire course."[9]
- The Rivalry among Competitors is high as there are many educational institutes and content providers sources available that compete on prices.

Taking into consideration all the forces, we understand that the profitability of the Education industry is Low.

Education Industry	Overall profitability is Low
Threat of New Entrants	High
Bargaining Power of Suppliers	High
Bargaining Power of Buyers	High
Availability of Substitutes	High
Rivalry among Competitors	High

In the Automotive industry,

- The Threat of New Entrants is low as there are high capital requirements to enter.
- There are plenty of suppliers that provide automotive parts. However, the costs of switching from one supplier to another could be moderate, which gives them moderate bargaining power.
- The main customers are individuals, commercial enterprises, and the government, who have the option of switching easily with low costs from one auto dealer or manufacturer to another. So, the Bargaining Power of Buyers is high.
- The substitute for personal vehicles is the public transportation. If there is a rise in fuel prices, people prefer public transportation. However, it cannot match the convenience of owning the vehicle. The Availability of Substitutes in the Automotive industry is low.
- The Rivalry among the Competitors is high as many compete over model, make, year of manufacture, and so on.

Taking into consideration all the forces, we understand that the profitability of Automotive industry is Moderate.

Automotive Industry	Overall profitability is Moderate
Threat of New Entrants	Low
Bargaining Power of Suppliers	Moderate
Bargaining Power of Buyers	High
Availability of Substitutes	Low
Rivalry among Competitors	High

Group Activity

You can find out the profitability of your industry.

1. Distribute the assessment questionnaire to all the key stakeholders in your organization. It contains a total of 26 questions.
2. To each statement in the assessment, assign a score between 1 and 6, depending on the extent to which you agree or disagree:
   1. Strongly Disagree
   2. Disagree
   3. Somewhat Disagree
   4. Somewhat Agree
   5. Agree
   6. Strongly Agree
3. Calculate the average score for each of the five forces.
4. Add the average scores to arrive at a final score. Compare the overall score with the following legend:
   between 5 and 10: High Industry Profitability
   between 11 and 22: Moderate Industry Profitability
   between 23 and 30: Low Industry Profitability

Assessment Questionnaire

		Your Score
	Threat of New Entrants	
1	Upfront capital investments are low	
2	Cost of switching from one supplier to another is low	

		Your Score
3	Incumbents don't have a strong power position	
4	There are a wide range of distribution channels available	
5	Ease of doing business is high	
6	Exit costs from industry are low	
7	Industry growth is rapid	
a)	Average Score	
	Bargaining Power of Suppliers	
8	Suppliers have better control over price	
9	Suppliers have strong dominance	
10	Switching costs from one supplier to another are high	
11	Supplier products are unique or highly differentiated	
12	There are few or no substitutes available for supplier products	
13	Supplier offers its products or services to multiple industries	
b)	Average Score	
	Bargaining Power of Buyers	
14	Buyer dominance is high	
15	Buyer can switch from one supplier product to another with low costs	
16	There are many undifferentiated products/services available	
c)	Average score	
	Availability of Substitutes	
17	There are many available substitutes for product/service	
18	It is easy to access or acquire substitutes	
19	Buyers would pay for lower quality substitutes available at lower price	
d)	Average Score	
	Rivalry among Competitors	
20	There are many incumbents in our industry	
21	Competition on price is intense among the incumbents	
22	Products are highly undifferentiated	
23	Switching costs from one incumbent product to another is low	
24	Industry growth is slow	
25	Cost of exiting the industry is high	
26	Incumbents fight to steal market share from one another	
e)	Average Score	
	Final Score: a + b + c + d + e	

Next, make a list of all the front-runners, entrepreneurs, and incumbents in your industry. Answer the questions as per the sheet below for each of them. Note that you can have a combined or separate sheet for each of them.

Front-runners/Incumbents/Entrepreneurs: _____	
1. What is the value provided to the customers? Is it through a new product, service, or experience, or a combination of all three?	
2. How does the customer interaction happen?	
3. How is the revenue generated?	4. What is the cost structure?

Customer Analysis

The success of a business depends upon the following three factors: the value your business offers to the customers, profits the customers bring into your business, and how you manage the relationships with your customers.

For firms to be successful in the digital age, it is important that they know their customers very well. Customers in the digital economy want:[10]

1. Personalized interactions at various points in the customer journey.
2. Transition from ownership to shared access.
3. Better customer experiences along with products and services.

Personalized interactions can be of two types:

First, providing customers flexibility to customize their products and services. A good example is NikeID or "Nike By You" which allows customers to create a unique shoe design as per their choice.

Second, providing relevant customer interactions by analyzing customer data. A good example is ginger.io, a mobile app that provides a platform that collects various samples and data points from patients undergoing stress, anxiety, and depression and accordingly offers them health and well-being recommendations or support, or even connects them to life behavior coaches.

In a shared access setup, a customer does not own any assets or resources, but gets access to it, whenever required. This unlocks the value of an underused asset and thus improves resource efficiency. A good example is Share Now, a German car-sharing company, formed from the merger between Car2Go and DriveNow. Customers using Share Now don't have to pay for parking, fuel, or insurance. All the rates are all-inclusive and are as flexible as pay-per-minute. They can drive whenever they want. This is unlike the car rentals where they have to pick up and drop off within specific opening hours. If they see a Share Now vehicle, they just need to hop in and drive. Also, they can park their cars anywhere within the city.[11]

Unlike traditional products, digital products offer better personalized customer experiences.

Following are the four capabilities that a digital product has that a traditional product does not:

- Monitor
- Control
- Optimize
- Autonomous[12]

Monitor enables a digital product to track the condition or environment in which it is operating.

Control enables a digital product to respond to specific changes in its condition or environment and allows users to customize it.

Optimize enables a digital product to apply algorithms and analytics to real-time or historical data collected from the condition or environment it operates in.

Autonomous enables a digital product to evaluate conditions or environment, make decisions, and coordinate with systems and other products to perform a task with minimum human input.

Each of these capabilities implies a level of increasing complexity. A digital product with control capability is also able to monitor, and a digital product cannot operate autonomously without having to monitor, control, and optimize.

Can you think of such a digital product existing, or can you invent one?

Digital services can be grouped into the following three categories:

1. Efficient services
2. Product-as-a-service
3. Service-replacing-products[13]

An *Efficient* service is based on the real-time data collected from products. For example, a vendor collecting real-time data from a coffee machine and proactively offering maintenance and repair services.

Offering LED lamps through a lighting-as-a-service model by Philips at Amsterdam's Schiphol airport is a good example of *Product-as-a-service*. Philips still owns the lamps and is responsible for maintenance, while the airport just pays for the energy consumption along with the service subscription fees.

Services-replacing-products include products that are replaced by software or virtualization. Streaming service offered by companies like Netflix is a great example of a service that has replaced physical products like DVDs.

Recently, I had a conversation with Devashri Dixit, the founder of Top-to-Toe Accessories, an online retailer of fashion accessories and imitation jewelry. She started her business in 2015 in London and has been able to steadily grow it over the years. Her business has a simple B2C model: procuring goods from Asian markets at a cheaper price and selling them in the European markets at a marked-up price. One of the reasons why her business is successful is her strong focus on customer needs. The performance metrics of her business are based not on the annual revenues earned but on the online behavior patterns of her customers such as the number of customers visiting her page, the number of customers engaged, the amount of time customers spend on a specific product, and the number of online conversions. She practically remembers all her customers; how often they buy and how much they buy. Because of her strong familiarity with her customer base, she provides good value to them by providing exclusive products catering to their needs. She is able to secure greater profits for her business because of value-based pricing and her superior negotiation skills. She is able to build good relationships and trust with her customers because of her sincerity and professionalism.

Most of the firms measure the success of their sales by revenues per market, revenues per product line or specific brands, revenues per channel, and so on. Rarely do they measure by observing the customer behavior.

A vegan packaged meals manufacturer named Vegoloka, based in Stockholm, Sweden, approached a small deli at Karolinska Hospital and convinced its owner to retail its products. Though the shop was small, it kind of enjoyed a monopoly in the hospital area as there were no food shops nearby. The hospital staff as well as visitors purchased their lunch from the deli that had limited vegan options. Since the Vegoloka products were specialty vegan meals, they were sold to the deli at a slightly higher price than others. Two weeks later, a sales representative from Vegoloka visited the deli to seek feedback on the products. The deli owner happily reported that though the profit margins and the number of new customers were low as compared to the other products, it had a healthy base of returning customers who purchased their products at least twice a week. The deli owner also offered to arrange a promotion campaign where they could attract new customers to taste a sample of its products. Thus, Vegoloka acquired its new order for the next two weeks from the deli. Had the deli owner looked at the scenario only from the profit margin perspective, Vegoloka might not have received its new order. However, since the center of focus was the customer buying behavior, it led to an altogether new business decision. It is known as the Customer Base Audit.

A *Customer Base Audit* is a systematic review of the buying behavior of a firm's customers using data captured by its transaction systems. The objective is to provide an understanding of how customers differ in their buying behavior and how their behavior evolves over time.[14]

Group Activity

1. You can make your own customer-base audit Excel sheet. Make the first column heading "List of Customers."
2. In the second and third columns, make headings "Revenues current year" and "Revenues previous year."
3. In the fourth and fifth columns, make headings "Profits current year" and "Profits previous year."
   If you sell products,
4. In the sixth and seventh columns, make headings "Interactions current year" and "Interactions previous year." Interactions include the number of times a customer interacted with you before making a purchase.

5. In the eighth and ninth columns, make headings "Purchases current year" and "Purchases previous year." Purchases mean the total revenues earned through a particular customer.

6. In the tenth and eleventh columns, make headings "Customer complaints current year" and "Customer complaints previous year."

List of customers	Revenues current year	Revenues previous year	Profits current year	Profits previous year	Interactions current year	Inter-actions previous year	Purchases current year	Purchases previous year	Complaints current year	Complaints previous year
Total										

If you sell services,

7. In the sixth and seventh columns, make headings as "Tickets raised current year" and "Tickets raised previous year."

8. In the eighth and ninth columns, make headings "Tickets resolved current year" and "Tickets resolved previous year."

9. In the tenth and eleventh columns, make headings "Number of Service Level Agreement (SLA) breaches current year" and "Number of SLA breaches previous year."

10. List your best customers (5 to 10) and vulnerable customers (5 to 10) primarily based on the value of purchase if you sell products and based on tickets raised if you sell services.

List of customers	Revenues current year	Revenues previous year	Profits current year	Profits previous year	Tickets raised current year	Tickets raised previous year	Tickets resolved current year	Tickets resolved previous year	Number of SLA breaches current year	Number of SLA breaches previous year
Total										

11. You can also use other parameters such as interactions and customer complaints for products and tickets resolved and SLA breaches for services.

12. Feel free to add more relevant column headings to the sheet based on your business requirements.

13. In your group, discuss the answers to the generic questions below for your best customer base:

    • What are the new needs or requirements of your customers?
    • What does their behavior tell you?
    • Are they profitable? How can you improve the profitability?
    • How do you connect with your customers?
    • How do you interact with them?
    • What new digital products and services would you like to offer to your customers? What experience would it create? What value would it add?

14. Now discuss the answers to the questions below for your vulnerable customer base:

    • What are the new needs or requirements of your customers?
    • What does their behavior tell you?
    • How do you connect with your customers?
    • How do you interact with them?
    • Are they profitable? If not, do you consider eliminating them?
    • If not, how would you restore the relationship with them?

Process Analysis

In every organization, the internal operations team is responsible for planning, organizing, and executing the work. The fundamental building block of internal operations is Process. A *Process* is a set of tasks to be performed in a defined sequence, which uses inputs to create outputs that are of great value to the customers and therefore to the organization itself.[15] Internal operations comprise multiple processes.

Figure 2.3 shows end-to-end internal operations comprising various processes and customer touch points such as:

    • Lead
    • Opportunity

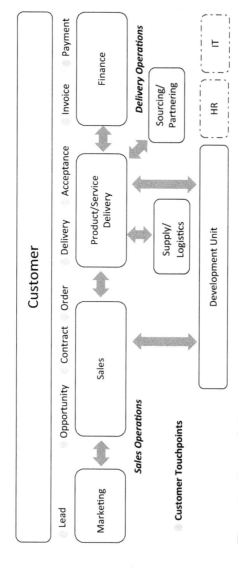

Figure 2.3 Internal Operations

- Contract
- Order
- Delivery
- Acceptance
- Invoice
- Payment

There are two types of processes:

- Intra functional
- Inter functional

Intra functional are the processes within a given function. For example, the processes within supply or within finance function. The Inter functional are the processes that exist between different functions. For example, the processes between sales and delivery or finance and delivery, and so on.

There are several processes in an organization. To prioritize them for automation, we use the following criteria:

1. *Impact on customer touchpoints*—the processes that involve interaction with customer at any given touchpoint in the customer journey must be given a high priority as they have a direct impact on the customer experience.
2. *Inter functional*—the processes that involve end-to-end interconnections between two or more different functions should be given higher priority than intra functional.
3. *Cost savings*—the processes that are costly to run must be given a higher priority.
4. *Complexity*—complex processes that involve lots of people, tools, and resource interactions should be given a higher priority.
5. *Time consumption*—the processes that are very lengthy and take hours or even days to complete should be given a higher priority.
6. *Manual intervention*—the processes that frequently need manual intervention to run should be given a higher priority.

7. *Repetitive*—the processes that are repetitive should be given a higher priority.

8. *Administrative*—the processes that are administrative should be given a higher priority.

Group Activity

- In the table below, list all the processes in your organization.

Process	Customer touchpoints	Inter functional	Costs	Complexity	Time consumption	Manual intervention	Repetitive	Administrative	Score
Process 1									
Process 2									
...									
...									
Process n									

- For each process, give a rating from 1 to 5 to each of the evaluation criteria:
  5—Very High
  4—High
  3—Moderate
  2—Low
  1—Very Low
- Then add up the final score for all the processes.

The processes with higher scores are to be given a high automation priority.

People Analysis

To enable digital transformation, it is essential to develop the right competence in people, which involves not only the development of digital skill sets but also a digital mindset. Competence development is a shared responsibility between an individual and the business. It is the responsibility of an individual to take ownership of one's competence, whereas the responsibility of the business to facilitate a learning environment.

A competence consists of three elements:

- Knowledge
- Skills
- Culture

Knowledge needs to be up-to-date, relevant, and easily available to people whenever they need it. To apply this knowledge in your daily work, you need skills, and to facilitate this, you need a culture of continuous learning and development.

Knowledge in an organization is divided into the following categories:

1. Product or service knowledge
2. Portfolio-wide knowledge
3. Digital technologies knowledge
4. Industry knowledge
5. Customer-specific knowledge

Product or Service knowledge comprises in-depth technical and functional know-how of a product or service. It includes the knowledge of features, advantages, and benefits it offers to the customers. The roles in an organization that need to be acquainted with such knowledge are Product Manager, Product Owner, Release Manager, Technical SME, and so on.

Portfolio-wide knowledge comprises the knowledge of all the current and future products and services available in the catalog. The roles in an organization that need to be acquainted with such knowledge are Portfolio Manager, Account Manager, Key Account Manager (KAM), Strategy Manager, Marketing Manager, and so on.

Digital technologies knowledge includes the knowledge of the latest emerging technologies such as AI, Automation, Data Science and Analytics, IoT, 5G, Cloud, XR, Metaverse, Blockchain, Gamification, and so on. People in technical roles need to develop technical expertise in one or more of the above technologies, while people in nontechnical roles only need to know an overview of these technologies and understand the business impact of each of them on different functions such as Operations, Sales, Finance, HR, Supply, and so on.

Industry knowledge includes the knowledge of industry where you sell your product or service. It also includes knowledge of adjacent industries where your product or service can be positioned. It contains the knowledge of industry profitability, industry size, value chain, digital landscape, disruptions, key people, and so on. All the employees in different roles in an organization are required to keep themselves updated with this knowledge.

Customer-specific knowledge includes the knowledge about the customer's business, key people, income statements, products, operational budgets, needs and requirements, and so on. The roles in an organization that need to be acquainted with such knowledge are Account Manager, KAM, Presales Manager, Service Delivery Manager, and so on.

Skills are divided into technical and nontechnical skills. An example of technical skills is data visualization tool such as Tableau or video editing tool such as Filmora. Nontechnical skills imply soft skills such as Leadership, Project Management, Negotiation, Communication, Strategy, and so on.

Some of the top technical skills for 2023[16] and beyond are:

- Python
- Cloud
- Cyber security
- Kubernetes and Terraform
- CI/CD and Automation
- Artificial Intelligence/Machine Learning (AI/ML)
- DevOps
- Data Science
- Linux
- Java

Some of the top nontechnical skills for 2023 and beyond are:

- Leadership
- Strategy
- Sales
- Project Management
- Negotiation
- Consulting
- Problem solving
- Communication

Skills such as Digital Marketing and UX/UI design which are a blend of technical and nontechnical ones are also some of the top skills for 2023 and beyond.

A *Culture* of continuous learning and development is an environment where:

- An individual takes one's own learning responsibility.
- Learning is a natural habit for individuals and teams.
- Learning and development is the top management priority.
- The management motivates and encourages people to learn and ensures there is a clear learning and development plan for everyone.
- The company invests in latest digital learning tools.
- There are regular check-ins and governance procedures in place.

Group Activity

1. Fill the knowledge matrix sheet below with the list of all the main jobs at your firm.
2. Map each job to the following knowledge areas: Product/Service knowledge, Portfolio-wide knowledge, Digital technologies knowledge, Industry knowledge, and Customer-specific knowledge. If a particular knowledge area is applicable to a specific job, then put "x." Otherwise leave blank.

Knowledge Matrix					
List of jobs	Product/ Service knowledge	Portfolio-wide knowledge	Digital technologies knowledge	Industry knowledge	Customer-specific knowledge
Job role 1					
Job role 2					
...					
...					
...					
Job role n					

3. Fill in the skills matrix sheet below with current and future technical and nontechnical skills.

Skills Matrix		
	Technical skills	Nontechnical skills
Current	• Skill 1 • Skill 2 • Skill... n	• Skill 1 • Skill 2 • Skill... n
Future	• Skill 1 • Skill 2 • Skill... n	• Skill 1 • Skill 2 • Skill... n

4. Discuss in your group the answers to the following questions:
   1. What is the new digital competence required?
   2. How to transition from current to new competence?
   3. What new jobs will be created in the future?
   4. What current jobs will be eliminated?
   5. To establish a learning culture, how do we make sure we:
      a. Encourage and motivate people to learn.
      b. Develop a clear learning plan or pathway for everyone.
      c. Access the latest digital learning tools.
      d. Establish a continuous learning check-in process.
      e. Set up a learning and development governance at all levels in your organization.

Data Analysis

Large amounts of data flow daily into a company's systems. Whenever a customer makes a purchase, new data points are generated. Whenever new operations are carried out, new sets of data are generated. A firm can make important business decisions based on data. Data Analysis involves three steps:

- Gathering data
- Analyzing data
- Communicating the analysis

Gathering data involves collecting or aggregating data from various sources.

Analyzing involves cleaning, sorting, structuring, and identifying various patterns in data.

Communicating involves sharing the analyzed data with respective stakeholders in an easy-to-visualize and presentable format using data visualization tools and techniques.

But before you begin the data analysis, it is important to understand the business objectives and have a clear data strategy.

To build an effective data strategy, there are following four capabilities to be considered:

- Fluidity
- Integration
- Real-time metrics
- Insights

Fluidity is the ability of the data, which is not private and confidential, to flow freely across various functions in an organization without being confined to silos.

Integration is the ability to aggregate and process both structured and unstructured data as an input to a task or operation.

Real-time metrics enable performance monitoring by viewing the important metrics or KPIs on the dashboard.

Insights enable a user to make certain predictions or operational decisions by observing patterns in the datasets.

In an organization, there are three types of data flows as shown in Figure 2.4:

1. Data flow at customer touchpoints
2. Data flow in between functions
3. Data flow within a function

The data flow at customer touchpoints can help a firm generate valuable insights about the customers, which its competitors may not. The data flow in between and within functions can help a firm generate valuable business insights which can help it make some important business decisions. This practice is known as *Data-driven decision making*. However, these insights may lose their value if not generated on time, thereby impacting the customer experience and the internal business operations.

The biggest challenge the incumbents face today is that the data stays in silos within one unit and does not flow freely across. Also, it is very difficult to integrate the data since it is confined to an IT tool/system or an application. This makes the generation of real-time metrics difficult, which results in a lack of availability of data insights on time.

Jaguar Land Rover, a British multinational automobile manufacturer, adopted a customer-centric approach from its traditional product-centric approach, ever since it was acquired by Tata Motors from Ford for $2.3 billion. It relied heavily on the Data Analytics. It began analyzing various touchpoints in the customer journey. A new car model was launched keeping the customers in the center during prelaunch and postlaunch phases. In the prelaunch phase, the collected customer data was provided as feedback to the design engineers and the commercial team to determine the right pricing strategy. After the launch, continuous feedback from customers was collected and analyzed using the data analytics tools. In the vehicle, many sensors continuously collected and monitored data and behaviors of the driver in real time, which was then used to make some important business decisions. For example, the sensors detected that urban customers spent more time in traffic jams than rural customers. This information resulted in creating a comfortable interior

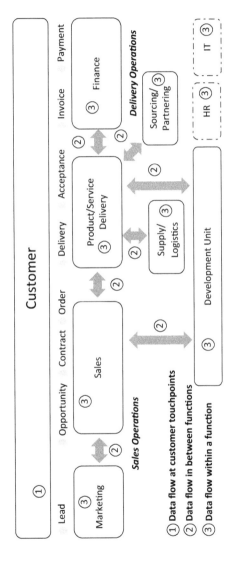

Figure 2.4 Three types of Data flows

seating for them. Jaguar Land Rover invested in a global (CRM) system, to better manage customer experiences and relationships. A customer coming to the end of the leasing contract would be given an invitation to test drive a successor car for leasing or an option to purchase a new car altogether. Customers who had just placed an order for a new customized car and waiting to take the delivery of it were provided information and updates throughout the entire lead time cycle of five months. The customers were provided photos of the car in the making at various manufacturing milestones. This kept them engaged throughout the process and ensured better customer loyalty.[17] This case is a good example of data flow between customer touchpoints, in between functions, and within a given function.

Group Activity

1. Using the sheet below, note down all the data flowing IN and OUT of the firm at various customer touchpoints.

Customer Touchpoints	Data flowing IN	Data flowing OUT
Lead		
Opportunity		
Contract		
Order		
Delivery		
Acceptance		
Invoice		
Payment		

2. Using the sheet below, note down all the data flowing in between various functions. Add or remove functions if needed.

Data flowing between functions	Delivery	Supply/ Logistics	Development unit	Finance	Marketing	Sourcing	HR	IT
Sales								
Delivery								
Supply/Logistics	X							
Development Unit	X	X						
Finance	X	X	X					
Marketing	X	X	X	X				
Sourcing	X	X	X	X	X			
HR	X	X	X	X	X	X		

3. Using the sheet below, note down all the data flowing within functions. Add or remove functions if needed.

Functions	Data flow
Sales	
Delivery	
Supply/Logistics	
Development unit	
Finance	
Marketing	
Sourcing	
HR	

4. In your group, for all the above three sheets, discuss the answers to the following generic questions for all the data flow types:

   a. Is the data sensitive? What portions of data are to be kept private and confidential?

   b. Is the data fluid? What are the systems, units, and tools impacted by this data currently? What could be impacted in the future?

   c. Is it easy to gather data from multiple sources? If not, what are the challenges? How can these challenges be overcome?

   d. What real-time metrics can be generated from this data? Who would be the target audience?

   e. Can this data generate valuable insights? What value can it add to the business?

IT Tools Analysis

An IT datacenter is the backbone of every company's operation, which hosts physical servers to manage the flow of data and information. The 1990s saw massive transformations with all the businesses from different industries becoming IT-centric. The businesses that were inherently IT were able to build effective and efficient datacenters. They even got into the business of leasing the datacenters to other businesses. However, the businesses that were non-IT, due to a lack of internal skills and IT competence, outsourced the building and management of datacenters to IT service providers. These service providers were responsible for the development and maintenance of different applications, platforms, and infrastructures. Most large incumbent firms fall into the latter category.

On average, an incumbent has at least 300 IT applications. Some are developed in-house, while some are sourced from different third parties and vendors. It is very cumbersome to manage such a large and complex IT landscape. In most cases, the IT operations are managed by multiple vendors. Thus, over a period, many under-utilized tools and applications get added to the landscape in an unorganized way. In *IT Tools Analysis*, we analyze which applications generate enough business value, using the nine important parameters:

1. *Criticality*—It considers how important is the tool in the business environment. Is it meeting the purpose or aligning with the business strategy? If you were to remove this tool from the environment, how much impact it could have on the business: high, low, or medium?
2. *Usage*—It considers how frequently is the tool used in daily business operations.
3. *Evolution*—It includes how the tool is evolving toward emerging technologies such as cloud security, automation, and so on, and if its future releases include these capabilities.
4. *Operational cost*—It includes the resources needed for maintenance and support and for continuous development, integration, upgrades, and updates.
5. *Security*—It considers the level of security the tool offers to protect data and information.

6. *Customization*—It considers how easily can one customize the tool to serve the business purpose.

7. *Reusability*—It considers how effectively can the tool that was originally developed for a specific business purpose be reused with some minor customization for a different business purpose.

8. *Interface*—It measures the ease of integrating the tool with other tools in the IT environment.

9. *Redundancy*—It considers if there are any similar tools available, either centrally or locally, that serve a similar business purpose.

Group Activity

1. In the sheet below, list all the IT tools in your organization.

Name of IT Tools	Criticality	Usage	Evolution	Operational costs	Security	Customization	Reusability	Interface	Redundancy	Score

2. Based on the impact it has on your business, give a rating from 1 to 5 for each of the evaluation criteria:
   5—very high impact
   4—high impact
   3—moderate impact
   2—low impact
   1—very low impact

3. For each tool, calculate the final score.

4. Then, discuss the answers to the following question in your group:
   a. What are the tools with lower and higher scores?
   b. What is the cost of maintaining them?
   c. Are they developed in-house or purchased from a third party?
   d. What can we do with them: phase out, replace, or migrate to cloud?

Summary

- Digital Maturity of an organization is modeled in two dimensions: New Business Adoption and Digital Technology Adoption.
- Industry Analysis involves determining the industry profitability based on Porter's five forces framework: Threat of New Entrants, Bargaining Power of Suppliers, Bargaining Power of Buyers, Availability of Substitutes, and Rivalry among Competitors.
- Customers in the digital economy want better experiences, personalization, and shared access to resources than ownership.
- The four capabilities of a digital product are: Monitor, Control, Optimize, and Autonomous.
- Digital services can be grouped into the following categories: Efficient services, Product-as-a-Service, and Service-replacing products.
- Customer Base Audit involves customer analysis based on buying behavior.
- Process Analysis is based on the following evaluation criteria: impact of customer touchpoints, inter-functional, costs, complexity, time consuming, manual intervention, repetitive, administrative.
- A competence comprises three elements: Knowledge, Skills, and Culture.
- To build an effective data strategy, there are four data capabilities to be considered: Fluidity, Integration, Real-time metrics, and Insights.
- In an organization, there are three types of data flows:
  1. Data flow at customer touchpoints
  2. Data flow in between functions
  3. Data flow within a function
- IT tools are analyzed based on the following criteria: Criticality, Usage, Evolution, Operational costs, Security, Customization, Reusability, Interface, Redundancy.

CHAPTER 3

Wanted Position and Strategic Priorities

After the Analysis phase, we start with the Definition phase, where we define a Digital Strategy.

A *Digital Strategy* comprises Wanted Position and Strategic Priorities. *Wanted Position* is a vision or objective where your firm wants to be in the next certain number of years. *Strategic Priorities* are the steps that determine how can you attain your wanted position.

Imagine you are currently living in London. You have a job with Europe's major investment banking firm at Canary Wharf. You have been working there for the last 5 years. You are impacted by the globalization happening around you and want to continue working in investment banking but not in London anymore. You want to pursue your Wall Street dream and move to New York in the next two years. Your job at Canary Wharf is your current situation. The Wall Street job is your *Wanted Position*. To pursue your dream job, you need to plan your next moves. You take a piece of paper and start writing down a list of things you want to do to make it happen.

- One, update your CV.
- Two, start exploring open positions.
- Three, apply to the open positions.
- Four, leverage your network to find connections on Wall Street.
- Five, assess your skills.
- Six, develop the ones you lack.

These are your strategic priorities. They tell you how you can land your dream job.

In 2002, Netflix launched an IPO, selling 5.5 million shares at $15 per share. It was making money from the mail-order DVD rentals. It soon realized that the market for DVD rentals would decline, and Internet streaming and video-on-demand (VOD) would be on the rise. In 2007, it started moving to Internet streaming and VOD business. Around the same time, lots of investments were made by the Communication Service Providers (CSP) in improving the quality of Internet infrastructure. This became the backbone of Netflix's business. New devices such as TVs, tablets, large-screen smartphones, and laptops sprung up providing users with a multiscreen viewing experience. Netflix faced competition from many firms who were operating in the Internet streaming industry such as cable television networks and production studios, who sought an exclusive agreement with the content providers. A big competitor of Netflix was Hulu, which was a joint venture between The Walt Disney Company, NBC Universal Television Group, and 21st Century Fox Inc. Hulu offered streaming services to subscribers in the United States and Japan for a monthly subscription fee of $7.99 to $11.99. By 2015, it had a subscriber base of nine million subscribers and had won exclusive rights to many popular television programs. Another competitor was Amazon, an e-commerce giant, that launched its video streaming services, leveraging its vast global user base, strong brand, and global IT infrastructure. Amazon differentiated itself from its competitors by giving users an option to buy or rent movies or television programs without a monthly subscription. Also, the services were accessible on a wide range of viewing platforms and streaming devices, from standard web browsers to game consoles such as Xbox and PlayStation.

By the beginning of 2016, Netflix estimated 74 million customers worldwide including both the domestic and international markets. In 2015, it had 3500 full-time employees and reported revenues of $6.78 billion. However, its growth in the domestic market in the United States was slow. To compensate for this, in 2016, Netflix formed its wanted position:

To increase the customer base in the markets worldwide.

To achieve the wanted position, it launched three strategic priorities:

1. Exclusive license agreements
2. Develop in-house content
3. Aggressive international market expansion strategy

Once the strategic priorities were formulated, the strategy execution began. House of Cards, a political drama, starring Kevin Spacey and Kate Mara, aired on Netflix in 2013, was the first content streamed through an exclusive licensing agreement. It secured exclusive licensing and distributing rights from some of the established Hollywood producers and studios such as The Walt Disney Company and its subsidiaries to gain exclusive streaming rights. It also acquired distribution licensing for feature films such as Beasts of No Nation, which was streamed on Netflix, the same day it was released in movie theatres.

To reduce its dependence on content providers, Netflix took a financial risk by producing its own content. As of late 2015, it began leasing studio space in Hollywood to begin filming episodes of television shows. In 2016, the company was expected to provide 600 hours of original programing, compared with 450 hours in 2015.

Netflix adopted an aggressive strategy to expand into new international markets. It entered new markets with limited services with limited time offers, which minimized the risk of offering a full service in an untested market. It utilized the data gained from these initial subscribers, mostly the type of programs they streamed, to create region-specific business models considering subscriber behavior more effectively in each market. To launch into the Japanese market, it partnered with Yoshimoto Kogyo, a Japanese talent agency, to produce exclusive local programs. Netflix funded the development of these programs in exchange for exclusive streaming rights for them for a set amount. To cater to the needs of the international local markets, Netflix was compelled to create content in the local market either by creating content of its own or by partnering with local content providers. In 2016, the spending on international content creation was $5 Billion.[1] Quite a large sum of investment for reaching its wanted position.

Group Activity

In this activity, we create a Wanted Position and Strategic Priorities. To create the former, we use the Digital Maturity Assessment as the baseline and to create the latter, we use the various analyses as the baseline.

Developing a Wanted Position

1. Refer to the Digital Maturity Assessment results.
2. In the sheet below, circle the current Digital Maturity level of your firm.

Time Frame: _____ months	Current Digital Maturity Level: 1/2/3/4/5	Future Digital Maturity Level: 1/2/3/4/5
New Business Adoption	Low/Medium/High	Low/Medium/High
Digital Technology Adoption	Low/Medium/High	Low/Medium/High

3. Circle the current New Business Adoption and Digital Technology Adoption levels.
4. Discuss in your group, the future New Business Adoption and Digital Technology Adoption levels you aspire to be at. Note them down in the sheet.
5. See the new maturity level that maps to your future New Business Adoption and Digital Technology Adoption levels from Figure 3.1.
6. Fill in the blank with the expected time frame to achieve the new maturity level.
7. Write a wanted position statement: "To be at level 2/3/4/5 from level 1/2/3/4 in __ months." (Circle the appropriate level and fill in the blank with the number of months)

Developing Strategic Priorities

8. Refer to the results of all the analyses: Industry, Customer, Process, People, Data, IT Tools.

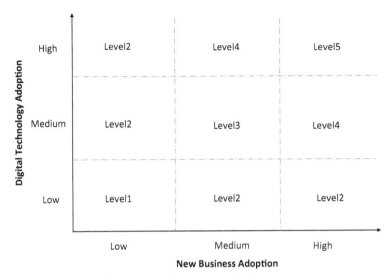

Figure 3.1 Digital Maturity Assessment levels

9. Discuss with your group the following open-ended questions:
   a. How can the current profitability of your industry be improved?
   b. How can the weaker forces from Porter's five forces framework be improved?
   c. How can the stronger forces from Porter's five forces framework be leveraged?
   d. What are the current and future needs of your customers?
   e. What new personalized experiences can you provide them?
   f. What new digital products and services can you offer them?
   g. Which processes can be automated?
   h. How can the lead times and costs be reduced?
   i. What is the overall business impact?
   j. How can we bridge the gap between current and future competence?
   k. What new learning programs do we need to implement?
   l. How can we create a learning culture?
   m. How can the data flowing at customer touchpoints add value?
   n. How can the data flowing in between the functions add value?
   o. How can the data flowing within the functions add value?
   p. How can we derive more value from the tools with higher scores?

10. List 3 preliminary strategic priorities corresponding to each of the analyses. Note them down in the sheet below.

Analysis	Preliminary Strategic Priorities	Final Strategic Priorities
Industry/Customer	1. 2. 3.	Best of 1,2,3
Process	4. 5. 6.	Best of 4,5,6
People	7. 8. 9.	Best of 7,8,9
Data	10. 11. 12.	Best of 10,11,12
IT Tools	13. 14. 15.	Best of 13,14,15

11. After discussing with your group, from the list of three Preliminary Strategic Priorities corresponding to each analysis, pick the best one to make the list of Final Strategic Priorities.
12. Refer to Chapter 6 to understand more about the practical application through case study.

Summary

- Use the Digital Maturity Assessment as the baseline for developing a Wanted Position.
- Use the outcome of different analyses: Industry, Customer, Process, People, Data, and IT tools as the baseline for developing Strategic Priorities.
- Wanted position statement: "To be at level" __ from level __ in "x" months.
- Corresponding to each analysis, make a list of Preliminary Strategic Priorities.
- Make the list of Final Strategic Priorities after reviewing with your team.

CHAPTER 4

Digital Strategy Execution

Though important, Strategy Execution is often a less traveled path in an organization. Once at a networking event in London, I met with a consultant from one of the top three strategy consulting firms across the globe. We were discussing many business topics over coffee and snacks. I was very impressed with her rich experience of consulting customers across different industries. She had the experience of working on strategy consulting projects with some of the top global brands throughout her career, where she was directly involved in formulating a digital strategy. I asked her about the common pain points she observed across different clients. She interestingly replied that her team works very closely with the clients, and they create one of the finest strategies for their businesses. But most often it only remains on the PowerPoint slides. The execution does not go as per expectations. Most firms spend lots of time and effort on digital strategy creation but very few achieve what they had originally intended to achieve. Strategy Execution is the biggest challenge the clients face. That's why we have changed the way we approach the clients. We position ourselves as continuous transformation partners and not just one-time solution providers. We want to be a part of our client's Strategy Execution too and not just creation.

Digital Strategy Execution contains two phases: Planning and Delivery. As shown in Figure 4.1, *Planning* phase includes Transformation Type Selection, Business Model Selection, Ecosystem Selection, Identification of Change Areas, Technology Mapping, Business Case, and Defining Metrics. The *Delivery* phase contains Dashboard Monitoring and Continuous Improvement.

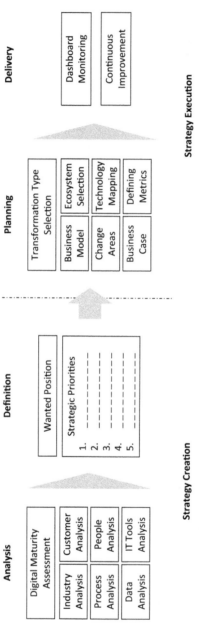

Figure 4.1 Digital Strategy Framework

Planning Phase

Transformation Type Selection

The first step of Planning phase of Strategy Execution is selecting a Transformation Type. There are three types of transformations: Core business, Support function, and Industry re-invention transformation.

Core business transformation involves redefining your mainstream business. A good example of core business transformation is Schibsted, a media incumbent based in Oslo, Norway. Schibsted realized that its high revenue-generating core business of print classified advertising was soon to decline. Its top management decided at the right time to transform the core business from print classified advertising to online classified advertising by offering a free online marketplace. Today, 80 percent of its revenue comes from commissions on sales from its consumer e-commerce platform.

Support function transformation means redefining functions such as Sales, Marketing, Finance, Accounting, Operations, HR, and so on, while keeping your core business intact. Most of the incumbents have started with the Support function transformation. Although Microsoft cannot be classified as an incumbent, the digitalization of its sales function is a good example. Earlier, the sales account executives at Microsoft had to deal with tons of software buyers, both individuals and enterprises. It was very difficult to understand the needs of every customer. Customer data was not organized due to which sales executives were unable to connect better with them. In 2021, Microsoft CEO Satya Nadella said that going forward every business process will be collaborative, powered by data and AI, and will bridge the digital and physical worlds. He brought a new culture of digitalization to Microsoft. Microsoft shifted its sales strategy from one-time purchases to software-as-a-service. They developed an in-house tool called "Daily Recommender" that offered recommendations and suggestions to salespeople. For example, algorithms detected that one customer company had spent a significant sum on software licenses and that 27 of its employees had recently interacted 34 times with Microsoft marketing materials. The tool thus enabled account executives to understand the customer needs better and focus on their pain points.[1]

Industry reinvention transformation means completely reinventing and redefining an industry by creating a new space that never existed before. Self-driving autonomous cars that run on electricity are a promising example. SAE International (formerly known as Society of Automation Engineers) has defined 0 to 5 levels of autonomy shown in the table below:[2]

Level	Driver	Vehicle
0: No Automation	Licensed driver with full attention and total control	No automation
1: Driver Assistance ("hands-on")	Licensed driver with full attention required	Semi-automated systems, like cruise control
2: Partial Automation ("pay attention")	Licensed driver with full attention required	Semi-automated systems, like steering, speed, and braking
3: Conditional Automation ("eyes off")	Licensed driver with ability to take control, if required	Primary driving functions are automated under some conditions
4: High Automation ("mind off")	No Licensed driver required (passengers OK)	Primary driving functions are automated under most conditions
5: Full Automation ("chauffeured")	No Licensed driver required (passengers OK)	Primary driving functions are automated under all conditions

It's 2024 and the level of autonomy reached for self-driving vehicles is somewhere between 2 and 3.[3]

Group Activity

Go through the flow chart in Figure 4.2 with your team and select the Transformation Type accordingly.

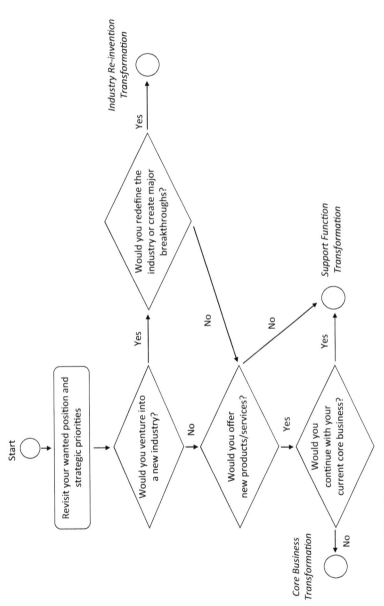

Figure 4.2 Flowchart

Business Model Selection

A business model explains how a company makes money by providing value to its customers. There are five widely adopted digital business models:

1. Platform based
2. Ad-supported
3. Freemium
4. Subscription based
5. Access over ownership

1. Platform based

   Back in 2007, before iPhone appeared on the scene, the five major mobile handset manufacturer's market shares were as shown in Figure 4.3.

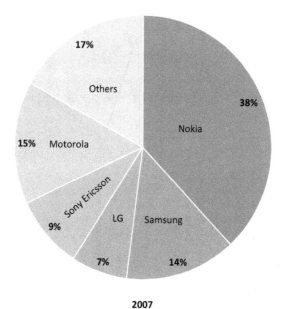

2007

Figure 4.3 Mobile manufacturer's market shares in 2007

Then in 2007, Apple launched the iPhone. In 2012, the market shares were as shown in Figure 4.4.

In 2015, the market shares were as shown in Figure 4.5.

Nokia who once upon a time dominated the industry disappeared from the scene. So, why were Apple and Samsung so successful, while Nokia failed? They became successful by exploiting the

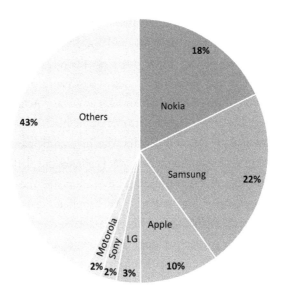

2012

Figure 4.4 Mobile manufacturer's market shares in 2012

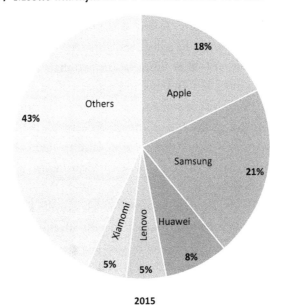

2015

Figure 4.5 Mobile manufacturer's market shares in 2015

power of "Platforms." Apple with its iPhone with iOS and Samsung with its Samsung Galaxy with Android created a "Platform," where they were able to bring together app developers on one side and app consumers on another, generating value for both groups.

If you make a comparison between the traditional business model and the platform based business model, we find that the traditional business model is linear, where one plays the role of a manufacturer, supplier, retailer, or consumer. Whereas in a platform based business model, one can play multiple roles such as owner, orchestrator, seller, and buyer. The owner is the controller of the platform who sets business rules and policies and decides who may participate in the platform and in what way. An orchestrator facilitates the platform. A seller creates offerings on the platform. A buyer purchases the offerings.

A shopping mall is a platform. Mall proprietor is the owner, stores are the orchestrators, brands are the sellers, and customers are the buyers.

Android is a platform. Google is the owner, handset manufacturers are the orchestrators, app developers are the sellers, and app users are the buyers.

Uber is a platform. Uber is the owner, vehicle owners are the orchestrators, vehicle drivers are the sellers, and Uber customers are the buyers. Vehicle owners can play a dual role as orchestrators and sellers.

Airbnb is a platform. Airbnb is the owner, property owners are the orchestrators and the sellers, and guests are the buyers.

In a traditional linear business, the two main assets to manage are the customer relationships and supplier relationships, whereas in the platform business one must manage information flowing in and out of the platform and interaction between the various players. Research has shown that when a platform enters the market of traditional linear business, the platform virtually always wins.[4]

2. Ad-supported

Firms with Ad-supported business models provide free content for users but charge the companies that host advertisements on their website or platform. Facebook and Google are good examples where they make revenue from ads while offering their product free of charge to the users. In 2022 Google's ad revenue amounted to $224.47 billion,[5] whereas Facebook generated $116.6 billion.[6]

3. Freemium

In the Freemium business model, the users get either a basic version of a product or service free of cost with the option of upgrading to an advanced paid version later. LinkedIn, Spotify, Dropbox, and Mailchimp are some of the popular examples.

4. Subscription based

In the subscription based business model, users must normally pay a monthly or annual fee for using a product or service. Netflix is a good example.

5. Access over ownership

In the Access over ownership model, you pay for the product or service, but you are not entitled to its ownership. You just get access to it. A good example is the Share Now car rental service as discussed in Chapter 2.

The transformation at Philips is a good example of adopting a new business model. When Frans van Houten became the CEO in April 2011, he was convinced that the company needed a significant transformation. He devised a transformation plan that was based on four strategic initiatives:

1. Radical portfolio choices
2. Accelerating growth and gaining competitive advantage
3. Transforming the operating model
4. Transformation of the company's culture and leadership

Philips made a critical decision to exit its sluggish consumer electronics business which included the television as it was making significant losses. Scott Cobb, principal at Southeastern Asset Management, which was Philips's biggest shareholder in 2013 commented:

Exiting consumer electronics for me is the real mark. These guys invented a lot of the consumer electronics we know- that is the part of Philips legacy. For them to say, "This is a business that is marginally profitable, struggling with declining revenue and does not have scale to compete," sends a massively strong signal that this company and its management are not the old Philips.

In 2014, Philips made a bold announcement to spin off its century-old lighting business from the rest of the company. Its new focus was to be an important player in the healthcare technology business. With an aging population, the rise of chronic diseases and increasing global wealth, the spending on healthcare was projected to rise significantly. Philips already had a strong brand position in both the hospital and home segments. The company had a great opportunity to connect the two segments more closely and approach healthcare in a more integrated manner. Frans van Houten introduced the concept of "health continuum" as a guiding principle in the transformation of healthcare.

He said:

Sick care focuses on diagnosis and treatment of people who have fallen ill. The vast majority of global healthcare spend is on diagnosis and treatment of people who are already sick. To create a breakthrough in health care, focus and resources need to shift to "healthy living" and "prevention" of diseases, as well as "early detection" and taking care of chronically sick people in lower-cost settings- the home. Not only will this be more cost-efficient, it can also improve the patient experience. Hospitals are designed for acute care and not necessarily the best option to take care of chronic patients.

The health continuum aimed at leveraging digital technology to offer more proactive and individualized care. Philips aimed at offering more integrated healthcare solutions, rather than standalone products. For example, an integrated approach to cancer care implies bringing together all the connected products and systems in radiology, pathology, the genomics diagnostics data of a patient, and a multidisciplinary team. It transformed its traditional way of doing business. Rather than selling an individual product to the hospital through a tender process, it aspired to form long-term partnerships with hospitals whereby Philips would provide an end-to-end technological solution at the client hospital. The benefit of this new approach would be that it would eliminate much waste from the healthcare system by optimizing workflows and asset utilization. The new business model of Philips included receiving payments based on performance improvements in the organization, not only in terms of financial results but also in terms of clinical outcomes and patient experience, thus aligning the performance goals of both Philips and its hospital clients.[7]

Group Activity

Discuss in your group the following questions if you are currently NOT using any of the above five business models.

1. Can we change our current business model to Platform based? What would be the pros and cons?
2. Do we want to own assets or resources? Can we change our current business model to Access over ownership? What would be the pros and cons?
3. Do we want to offer free products and services to our customers perpetually? If yes, then can we change our business model to Ad-supported? What would be the pros and cons?
4. Do we want to offer free products and services to our customers initially and charge later for premium upgrades? If yes, can we change our business model to Freemium? What would be the pros and cons?
5. Can we change our business model to Subscription based? What would be the pros and cons?
6. Can we combine two or more of the above five business models? What would be the pros and cons?
7. Can we continue with our current business model? What are the pros and cons?
8. Is there a new business model, besides the above 5, that we can adopt? What are the pros and cons?

Discuss in your group the following questions if you are currently using any one of the above five business models.

1. What value is your current business model generating?
2. Can we change our current business model to either of the other four? What would be the pros and cons?
3. Can we combine our current business model with any of the other four? What would be the pros and cons?
4. Is there a new business model we can adopt? What are the pros and cons?

Ecosystems

To succeed in the digital age, it is sometimes important for firms to collaborate or partner with one another. That's where the ecosystems play a very important role. An ecosystem is defined as a group or cohort with certain business objectives, where people seek and share knowledge and information with one another. Future of Work will be largely dependent on a firm's ability to work in ecosystems.[8] A McKinsey report suggests that by 2025, ecosystems will generate $60 trillion in revenue, which will constitute 30 percent of global sales in that year.[9] Boston Consulting Group found that the use of the word "ecosystem" in large companies' annual reports had grown 13-fold over the last decade and that firms using and acting on it grew much more rapidly than those that didn't.[10]

There are two types of players in an ecosystem: a Pioneer and a Follower, where both mutually benefit from each other. Pioneers play a leadership role in the ecosystem, keeping together firms with different expertise and business models, whereas followers with their unique strengths and expertise, add and extract value from the ecosystem. Ecosystems exist across industries and within an industry. In an ecosystem across industries, pioneers and followers share value through a common collaboration. In an ecosystem within an industry, a firm collaborates with its competitors, partners, or even customers to derive more value from each other.

A good example of an ecosystem within and across industries is Mediacorp, a national broadcaster based in Singapore, which was a wholly owned subsidiary of Temasek Holdings Limited. It had an ambition to transition to a national media network from a national broadcaster. To do so, it took a lead role as an ecosystem pioneer, bringing together different players in the media industry. It set up an initiative called Mediacorp Partner Network (MPN) to bring together brands such as ESPN (sports broadcaster), mothership (online news website in Singapore), Popcorn (movie app), the Asianparent (largest parenting website in Asia), Vice (youth media company), YouTube (online video sharing and social media platform), and 99.co (real estate agency) in its partner network.[11] Besides MPN, Mediacorp also has Owned and Operated (O&O) platforms such as CNA, Today, 8 world, Berita for news, meWatch for video-on-demand streaming, meListen for online radio streaming, meRewards for rewards, cashback, perks, promos, and Bloomr.sg for content creation.[12] In April 2019, Mediacorp partnered with Wattpad, the online storytelling platform to screen its stories across Singapore.[13] In Oct 2021, Mediacorp launched SocialHub, a new self-service platform that connects marketers and media agencies to social media talents, influencers, celebrities, digital content creators, and talents from partner agencies.[14] Mediacorp in partnership with Lazada, one of Southeast Asia's leading e-commerce platforms, developed a collaboration for its National Day mega sale from August 8th to 10th, 2020. Mediacorp personalities launched a game show called "Guess It," where the audience was asked to guess the prices of the featured products.[15]

Digiculum, an ecosystem orchestration company, based in Stockholm, Sweden, ran an ecosystem pilot in 2021 for 6 months, with some of the top global Nordic brands. It brought the Learning and Development (L&D) teams from each of these companies together into the ecosystem. The participants were addressed as "members." The members were expected to share success stories, best practices, and new ways of working with others. The ecosystem was all about sharing and seeking value. Whenever a member wanted to seek help, it had to generate a request. The request could be an insight on any topic related to L&D. It could be benchmarking a process or a practice. Or, it could be a consulting support, one member needed from the other members.

One member wanted consulting support on how to measure the success of the upskilling and reskilling learning programs. It created a request on the ecosystem. Another one responded to the request as it had been successfully tracking the ROI on learning programs based on Kirkpatrick's model[16] and was happy to share the best practices with the requestor. Digiculum facilitated a deeper knowledge-sharing workshop between both members. At the ecosystem monthly review meeting, the knowledge-sharing experiences between the two members were shared with others.

One member wanted to seek best practices and new perspectives on building a robust Learning Management System (LMS) platform-like space on SharePoint. It created a request. Every member of the ecosystem responded to the request. A three-hour brainstorming workshop was then scheduled. It was a successful workshop where the requestor member received useful feedback and insights from others.

At the end of the six-month pilot period of the ecosystem, feedback was collected from the different members. One such feedback was that the interaction was very simple and personal. It happened face-to-face through Microsoft Teams, as opposed to other impersonal forms such as tools or platforms. It was a value add for everyone.

This ecosystem could scale up to more companies. There could also be industry-focused ecosystems connecting different players from different industries such as banking, telecommunications, retail, and so on.

How do you know which ecosystem is beneficial for you? Should you be a follower or a pioneer? The selection of an ecosystem largely depends on the pioneers and followers that bring value to your business. First, you must know your digital strategic priorities very well and then do due diligence on all the ecosystems available using the following five criteria:

- Objective
- Differentiation
- Trust
- Governance
- Flexibility

Your firm can interview the existing members of the prospective ecosystem and get information about the above criteria.

Objective involves finding the main purpose of the pioneers and followers to join the ecosystem. You can start with the following questions:

What innovations to bring?

What business problems are they trying to solve?

How closely the objective of the ecosystem matches your firm's purpose to join the ecosystem?

Differentiation involves understanding the unique capability each player is bringing to the ecosystem. *Trust* explores the amount of mutual confidence and respect each player has for one another. Your firm must decide how well would you trust each of the members of the prospective ecosystem.

Governance describes how all the players can solve issues with utmost cooperation and monitor the progress and performance of the ecosystem.

Flexibility means how quickly can each player adapt to the changes.

Group Activity

1. Using the sheet below, list down all the ecosystems that you want to be a part of or want to initiate.

Ecosystems	Objective	Differentiation	Trust	Governance	Flexibility	Score
Ecosystem 1						
Ecosystem 2						
...						
...						
Ecosystem n						

2. Rate the overall objective using the rating:
   1—Very low match
   2—Low match
   3—Moderate match
   4—High match
   5—Very high match
3. Rate the overall differentiation with the following rating:
   1—Very low differentiation
   2—Low differentiation
   3—Moderate differentiation
   4—High differentiation
   5—Very high differentiation
4. Rate the overall trust on the following rating:
   1—Very low trust
   2—Low trust
   3—Moderate trust
   4—High trust
   5—Very high trust
5. Rate the overall governance with the following rating:
   1—Very low governance
   2—Low governance
   3—Moderate governance
   4—High governance
   5—Very high governance

6. Rate the overall flexibility with the following rating:
   1—Very low flexibility
   2—Low flexibility
   3—Moderate flexibility
   4—High flexibility
   5—Very high flexibility
7. Add the final score for all the ecosystems. Select the one with the highest score.

Identification of Change Areas

Identification of Change Areas largely depends on the Strategic Priorities you set for your business, which eventually helps you to reach your Wanted Position. There are many areas in your business that you would like to transform in your company. However, priority must be given to the ones that align with your Strategic Priorities.

Let us consider a fictitious story of Nirmiti Creations, a retail store business that sells fashion accessories and imitation jewelry to customers in Europe. It currently operates its business through an e-commerce website and a Facebook page. Many customers from different parts of Europe visit the page and browse through the various products in the product catalog. Nirmiti Creations decided to use the Digital Transformation to increase revenue, reduce costs, and improve customer experience. It listed the following five Strategic Priorities:

1. Offer personalized experiences
2. Expand customer base
3. Introduce new products and services
4. Achieve cost efficiency
5. Develop digital competence

For the Strategic Priority—Offer personalized experiences, the Change Area would be building a database that stores customer personas, buying patterns and behaviors, and purchasing history. So, whenever the customers log in next time, they are offered a personalized experience by promoting the most likely products.

For the Strategic Priority—Expand customer base, the Change Area would be generating the correct leads and marketing the products to the right customers via digital channels and social media such as Instagram, Twitter, LinkedIn, and Facebook.

For the Strategic Priority—Introduce new products and services, the Change Area would be an introduction of a new home delivery service.

For the Strategic Priority—Achieve cost efficiency, the Change Area would be the digitalization of supply chain.

And, for the Strategic Priority—Develop digital competence, the Change Area would be building new digital skills such as Digital Marketing and UX design.

Strategic Priorities	Change Areas
Offer personalized experiences	Build a database
Expand customer base	Lead generation and marketing
Introduce new products and services	New home delivery service
Achieve cost efficiency	Digitalize supply chain
Develop digital competence	Build new digital skills

Thus, for every Strategic Priority, there should be at least one Change Area mapped.

My last role during my 11-year tenure with a leading telecommunications incumbent was the Head of Competence Readiness for the solution area: Business Support Systems (BSS). The global BSS team comprised 5000+ employees. I was responsible for the competence development for all of them. BSS competence development programs were running in silos in different market areas. I had to streamline these programs centrally for which I made a competence readiness plan and got it approved by the BSS leadership team.

There were three main strategic priorities:

1. Improve current BSS competence.
2. Develop future BSS competence.
3. Develop a continuous learning culture.

Improving current BSS competence involved the following Change Areas:

1. BSS competence development program: ensuring that all BSS employees are trained on the BSS portfolio such as billing, charging, order care, catalog manager, and CRM

2. Communication between Product Managers and Presales Managers: ensuring that the Product Managers are aligned with the latest product releases with Presales Managers in the different market areas.

Developing future competence involved the following Change Areas:

1. Build competence in Cloud
2. Build competence in AI

Developing a continuous learning culture involved the following Change Areas:

1. Starting a bi-weekly global knowledge-sharing session with BSS employees globally
2. Develop KPIs and monitor the progress of the competence readiness program

Strategic Priorities	Change Areas
Improve current BSS competence	• BSS competence development program • Communication between Product managers and Presales managers
Develop future BSS competence	• Build competence in Cloud • Build competence in AI
Develop a continuous learning culture	• Bi-weekly knowledge-sharing sessions • Develop KPIs and monitor the progress

Group Activity

1. Use the sheet below. Add the strategic priorities.

Strategic Priorities	Change Areas	Technology Mapping	Business Value	Cost of Change	KPIs
1.					
2.					
3.					
4.					
5.					

2. Discuss in your group the Change Areas to be mapped to each of the Strategic Priorities.

There needs to be at least a Change Area mapped to each of the Strategic Priorities.

Refer to the fictitious case study in Chapter 6 for more details.

Technology Mapping

Once the Change Areas are identified, the next step is to find out which digital technology to use to enable the change. New emerging digital technologies play a very important role in Digital Transformation as they enable:

- Scope
- Scale
- Speed

Scope implies offering multiple products or services to a single customer. *Scale* implies offering a single product or service to multiple customers. *Speed* implies delivering products or services faster to the customers.

Some of the popular emerging technologies that can be incorporated into your business today are AI, Automation, Data Science and Data Analytics, IoT, 5G, AR/VR, Cloud, Metaverse, Blockchain, and Gamification. Refer appendix for more details.

Considering the Nirmiti Creations story, following are the digital technologies mapped to each of the Change Areas:

Strategic Priorities	Change Areas	Technology Mapping
Offer personalized experiences	Build a database	AI, Cloud
Expand customer base	Lead generation and marketing	AI
Introduce new products and services	New home delivery service	Automation
Achieve cost efficiency	Digitalize supply chain	Automation
Develop digital competence	Build new digital skills	Digital Marketing, UX design

For the Change Area—Build a database that stores customer personas, buying patterns and behaviors, and purchasing history, AI and Cloud would be the best digital technologies to be used. Public Cloud providers such as AWS, Azure, and Google Cloud can provide the database to store information such as:

- Customer persona: name, age, address, social security number, gender, and preferences
- Buying patterns: total number of visits on the website, date and time of visits, frequency of visits, physical location of visits, number of products clicked, time spent on each product, and sales conversions
- Purchasing history: date and time of previous purchases, mode of payment used, customer experience, reviews, and recommendations

AI can then run algorithms on the above data to provide users with product recommendations and discounts.

For the Change Area—Generating the correct leads and marketing products to the right customers via digital channels and social media, AI would be the best digital technology to be used. Based on the business goals of the company and previous customer profiles, AI algorithms would scan the Internet and recommend potential customers or leads. It can also market specific products to them with offers and discounts.

For the Change Area—New home delivery service, Automation would be the best digital technology to be used. Once the user purchases using the home delivery option, an automatic notification will be sent to the next available delivery agent who can pick up the product from the warehouse and deliver it physically to the home address.

For the Change Area—Digitalize supply chain, Automation again would be the best digital technology to be used. Automation can digitalize the supply chain by eliminating manual processes in supply, logistics, and inventory management.

For the Change Area—Build new digital skills, training programs could be arranged for the employees on technologies such as Digital Marketing and UX Design.

Group Activity

1. Continue using the sheet below, with Strategic Priorities and Change Areas added.

Strategic Priorities	Change Areas	Technology Mapping	Business Value	Cost of Change	KPIs
1.					
2.					
3.					
4.					
5.					

2. Discuss in your group the digital technologies to be mapped to the Change Areas and add them under the Technology Mapping column.

There needs to be at least one Technology mapped to each of the Change Areas.

Refer to the fictitious case study in Chapter 6 for more details.

Business Case

Once the Technology Mapping is done, the next step is to build a Business Case. Business case has two components:

- Business Value
- Cost of Change

Business Value can be broadly categorized in terms of Increased Revenue, Cost Reduction, and Improved Customer Satisfaction.

Cost of Change helps us estimate the cost required to enable this Change Area by calculating the implementation costs of each of the digital technologies.

In the case of Nirmiti Creations, following are the business values, each of the Change Areas and mapped technologies provide:

- Building a database using Cloud and AI can provide Improved Customer Satisfaction.
  The promotional offers and discounts given to customers based on their buying preferences can increase customer loyalty toward the brand.
- Use of AI to expand customer base can result in Increased Revenue.
  Since AI would generate the correct leads and target the right customers, the chances of sales conversions would increase, thereby increasing revenue.

- Using Automation to offer new online delivery services can result in Cost Reduction and Increased Revenue.
  Automation would eliminate unwanted processes and thus enable cost reduction. It would help the introduction of a new automated online delivery service, which can enable increased revenue.
- Using Automation to digitalize the supply chain can result in Cost Reduction.
  Digitalization of the supply chain using Automation would eliminate waste, improve efficiency, and thus enable cost reduction.
- Developing digital competence can enable employees to be equipped with the latest knowledge and expertise, which can indirectly contribute to Increased Revenue and Improved Customer Satisfaction.

Strategic Priorities	Change Areas	Technology Mapping	Business Value
Offer personalized experiences	Build a database	AI, Cloud	Improved Customer Satisfaction
Expand customer base	Lead generation and marketing	AI	Increased Revenue
Introduce new products and services	New home delivery service	Automation	Cost Reduction, Increased Revenue
Achieve cost efficiency	Digitalize supply chain	Automation	Cost Reduction
Develop digital competence	Build new digital skills	Digital Marketing, UX design	Increased Revenue, Improved Customer Satisfaction

The Business Value and Cost of Change can be quantified as Very High, High, Medium, Low, or Very Low.

Following are the estimated costs of change for each of the mapped technologies:

Strategic Priorities	Change Areas	Technology Mapping	Business Value	Cost of Change
Offer personalized experiences	Build a database	AI, Cloud	Improved Customer Satisfaction	High
Expand customer base	Lead generation and marketing	AI	Increased Revenue	Medium
Introduce new products and services	New home delivery service	Automation	Cost Reduction, Increased Revenue	Low

Strategic Priorities	Change Areas	Technology Mapping	Business Value	Cost of Change
Achieve cost efficiency	Digitalize supply chain	Automation	Cost Reduction	Medium
Develop digital competence	Build new digital skills	Digital Marketing, UX design	Increased Revenue, Improved Customer Satisfaction	Medium

Group Activity

- Continue using the sheet below, with Strategic Priorities, Change Areas, and Technologies added.

Strategic Priorities	Change Areas	Technology Mapping	Business Value	Cost of Change	KPIs
1.					
2.					
3.					
4.					
5.					

- Discuss in your group the Business Value and the Cost of Change for each of the Change Areas.

There could be more than one business value mapped to each of the Change Areas.

Based on the Cost of Change and the Business Value, the following business decisions can be made:

Business Value	Cost of Change	Business Decisions
Very High/High	Very Low/Low/Medium	Enable the Change Area
Very Low/Low	High/Very High	Do not enable the Change Area
Medium	High/Very High	Further due diligence
Very High/High	Very High/High	Further due diligence
Very Low/Low/Medium	Very Low/Low/Medium	Further due diligence

Metrics

Metrics play an important role in monitoring the progress of Strategy Execution. While defining Strategic Priorities, it is very important to define the key metrics as clearly and concretely as possible.

Going back to the example of Nirmiti Creations, the following metrics can be used for each Strategic Priority:

For the Strategic Priority—Offer personalized experiences, metrics can be:

- Overall customer satisfaction
- Percent of recommended products purchased

Customer satisfaction can be measured from sources such as review scores from social media or direct feedback based on the data collected and processed by AI. A higher percentage of recommended products purchased provides a good indication of improved customer satisfaction.

For the Strategic Priority—Expand customer base, the metrics can be:

- Number of new customers visiting the website current month
- Percent of new customers making a purchase

The latest and real-time values can be acquired by the data collected and processed by AI.

For the Strategic Priority—Introduction of new products and services, the metrics can be:

- Number of new products introduced current month
- Percent Increased revenue

A comparison between the revenue before and after implementation of Automation can provide the percentage of increased revenue.

For the Strategic Priority—Achieve cost efficiency, the metrics can be:

- Percent Cost reduction
- Number of free man hours per week

A comparison between the costs before and after the implementation of Automation can provide the percentage of cost reduction. Number of free man hours per week is the measurement of average free time per employee enabled due to Automation.

And for the Strategic Priority—Develop digital competence, the metrics can be:

- Number of employees completing training program per month
- Employee feedback score

Employee feedback scores can be collected using an online survey after the completion of a particular learning course.

The table below shows a mapping between Strategic Priorities, Change Areas, Technology Mapping, Business Value, Cost of Change, and KPIs.

Strategic Priorities	Change Areas	Technology Mapping	Business Value	Cost of Change	KPIs
Offer personalized experiences	Build a database	AI, Cloud	Improved Customer Satisfaction	High	• Overall customer satisfaction • % of recommended products purchased
Expand customer base	Lead generation and marketing	AI	Increased Revenue	Medium	• Number of new customers visiting the website current month • % of new customers making a purchase
Introduce new products and services	New home delivery service	Automation	Cost Reduction, Increased Revenue	Low	• Number of new products introduced current month • % Increased revenue
Achieve cost efficiency	Digitalize supply chain	Automation	Cost Reduction	Medium	• % Cost reduction • Number of free man hours per week
Develop digital competence	Build new digital skills	Digital Marketing, UX design	Increased Revenue, Improved Customer Satisfaction	Medium	• Number of employees completing training per month • Employee feedback score

For every Strategic Priority, there needs to be at least one metric or KPI. KPI stands for Key Performance Indicator. It contains:

- Statement
- Target
- Performance Indicators

Imagine a consulting firm that has 100 contracts with a global customer. The payment credit period is 90 days. Its management team decided to renegotiate the credit period from 90 days to 60 days, within a time frame of 2 years. The approximate plan is to negotiate around 50 contracts in the current year and the remaining 50 next year. Then:

Strategic Priority would be to renegotiate the credit period to 60 days within one year.

The KPI statement would be: #Number of contracts renegotiated
KPI target could be: 45–50 within next 1 year

Performance Indicators could be:

- *Off-track* for less than 40 contracts negotiated
- *On-track* for 40 to 50 contracts negotiated
- *Stretch* for contracts above 50 negotiated

The detailed definition of KPIs in the Nirmiti Creations example is as follows:

Strategic Priorities	KPI Statement	Target	Performance Indicators
Offer personalized experiences	1. Overall customer satisfaction	Score above 6 on the scale of 1 to 10	Off-track—Score 5 and below On-track—Score between 6 and 8 Stretch—Scores 9 and 10
	2. % of recommended products purchased	Above 10%	Off-track—below 10% On-track—between 10% and 15% Stretch—above 15%
Expanding customer base	1. Number of new customers visiting the website current month	Between 25 and 50	Off-track—below 25 On-track—between 25 and 50 Stretch—above 50
	2. % of new customers making a purchase	Above 50%	Off-track—below 50% On-track—between 50% and 75% Stretch—above 75%
Introduction of new products and services	1. Number of new products introduced current month	Between 5 and 10	Off-track—below 5 On-track—between 5 and 10 Stretch—above 10

Strategic Priorities	KPI Statement	Target	Performance Indicators
	2. % Increased revenue	Between 25% and 40%	Off-track—below 25% On-track—between 25% and 40% Stretch—above 40%
Achieve cost efficiency	1. % Cost reduction	Between 35% and 50%	Off-track—below 35% On-track—between 35% and 50% Stretch—above 50%
	2. Number of free man hours per week	Between 4 and 7 hours	Off-track—below 4 On-track—between 4 and 7 Stretch—above 7
Develop digital competence	1. Number of employees completing training per month	Between 7 and 10	Off-track—below 7 On-track—between 7 and 10 Stretch—above 10
	2. Employee feedback score	Score above 6 on the scale of 1 to 10	Off-track—Score 5 and below On-track—Score between 6 and 8 Stretch—Scores 9 and 10

Group Activity

1. Continue using the sheet below with Strategic Priorities, Change Areas, Technology Mapping, Business Value, and Cost of Change added.

Strategic Priorities	Change Areas	Technology Mapping	Business Value	Cost of Change	KPIs
1.					
2.					
3.					
4.					
5.					

2. Discuss in your group, the KPIs for each of the Strategic Priorities.

There could be more than one KPI mapped to each of the Strategic Priorities.

Delivery Phase

Once the Planning phase is completed, the Delivery phase begins. The two important steps are Dashboard Monitoring and Continuous Improvement. Both should happen simultaneously.

Dashboard Monitoring

Dashboards are central hubs for multiple reports that provide easy access to various datasets simultaneously.[17] Unlike scorecards, dashboards monitor KPIs in real time. An ideal time interval for dashboard updates is 15 minutes. It is customizable as per the business requirements. The health of the KPIs can be either indicated by red, amber, green (RAG) colors or states such as Off-track, On-track, or Stretch. Users can add or remove any additional state if needed. If KPIs are green, then things are on track. If KPIs are amber, it is a warning sign. They can either improve or become worse. An effort should be made to move them to green. If they are red, it means things are off-track. Prompt actions need to be taken as per the SLA to restore them to amber and eventually green. If the KPIs remain red for a long amount of time, it a matter of concern for the management. Immediate actions should be taken to evaluate the execution steps or even re-defining the Strategic Priorities.

Let us revisit the story of Nirmiti Creations. Following was the current state of the KPIs as shown in the table at a certain time. The performance indicators used are Off-track, On-track, and Stretch.

Strategic Priorities	KPI statement	Target	Performance Indicators	Current state
Offer personalized experiences	1. Overall customer satisfaction	Score above 6 on a scale of 1 to 10	Off-track—Score 5 and below On-track—Score between 6 and 8 Stretch—Scores 9 and 10	6
	2. % of recommended products purchased	Above 10%	Off-track—below 10% On-track—between 10% and 15% Stretch—above 15%	8%

Strategic Priorities	KPI statement	Target	Performance Indicators	Current state
Expanding customer base	1. Number of new customers visiting the website current month	Between 25 and 50	Off-track—below 25 On-track—between 25 and 50 Stretch—above 50	20
	2. % of new customers making a purchase	Above 50%	Off-track—below 50% On-track—between 50% and 75% Stretch—above 75%	25%
Introduction of new products and services	1. Number of new products introduced current month	Between 5 and 10	Off-track—below 5 On-track—between 5 and 10 Stretch—above 10	12
	2. % Increased revenue	Between 25% and 40%	Off-track—below 25% On-track—between 25% and 40% Stretch—above 40%	20%
Achieve cost efficiency	1. % Cost reduction	Between 35% and 50%	Off-track—below 35% On-track—between 35% and 50% Stretch—above 50%	25%
	2. Number of free man hours per week	Between 4 and 7 hours	Off-track—below 4 On-track—between 4 and 7 Stretch—above 7	5
Develop digital competence	1. Number of employees completing training per month	Between 7 and 10	Off-track—below 7 On-track—between 7 and 10 Stretch—above 10	11
	2. Employee feedback score	Score above 6 on a scale of 1 to 10	Off-track—Score 5 and below On-track—Score between 6 and 8 Stretch—Scores 9 and 10	7

The management of the retail store can decide how they want to view the KPIs on the dashboard. Either they can choose full view or customized view.

The full view of the KPIs on the dashboard would be as per shown in Figure 4.6.

The management can also customize the KPI views. Figure 4.7 shows the customized ones with off-track status.

Continuous Improvement

Continuous Improvement should be made to KPIs that are amber or red or showing off-track status until they become green or show on-track

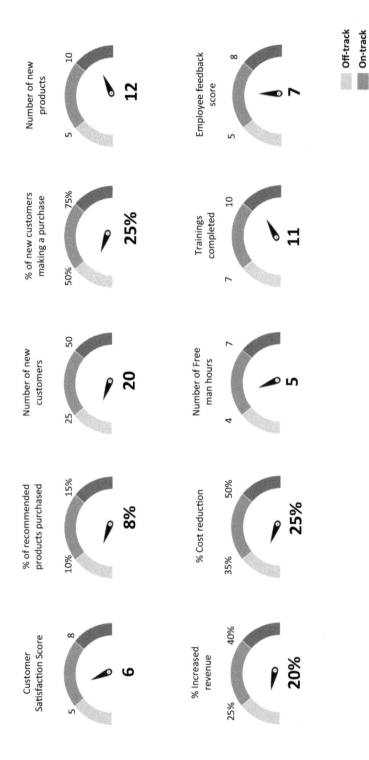

Figure 4.6 KPI dashboard

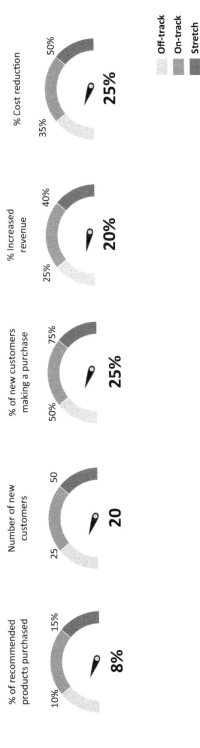

Figure 4.7 Customized KPIs with off-track status

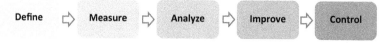

Figure 4.8 **DMAIC**

status. One of the widely used continuous improvement processes is DMAIC:

- Define
- Measure
- Analyze
- Improve
- Control

In *Define*, the problem is stated. The important question to ask is—Who are the key people involved?

In *Measure*, the performance metrics are identified. The important question to ask is—How is the success measured?

In *Analyze*, the root cause of the problem is identified. The important question to ask is—What impact does it have on business?

In *Improve*, a solution to the problem is tested and implemented. The important question to ask is—Are there any costs or risks involved in implementing the solution?

In *Control*, the changes are monitored over time. The important question to ask is—Is the implemented solution stable and sustainable?

In the story of Nirmiti Creations, the off-track KPIs are:

- KPI 1# Percent of recommended products purchased
- KPI 2# Number of new customers visiting the website current month
- KPI 3# Percent of new customers making a purchase
- KPI 4# Percent increased revenue
- KPI 5# Percent cost reduction

After a detailed analysis of the problems, it was found that:

- For KPI 1, more details were needed to understand the customer preferences for the AI algorithm to make correct product recommendations to them.
- For KPI 2, the website was not promoted and marketed enough.
- For KPI 3, the website was in English only and didn't have a local language version for different European markets. Hence it was difficult for the local customers to connect with the brand.
- For KPI 4, the main reasons for less revenue were that fewer customers were visiting the website, product portfolio lacked variety, and the preferences of local customers were not taken into consideration.
- For KPI 5, supply and logistics resulted in higher costs, and the processes were not automated.

Following were the improvement solutions suggested:

- For KPI 1, customers to fill out an online survey to understand their preferences better. Incentives and discount coupons to be offered to those who do so.
- For KPI 2, additional budget for aggressive promotions of the website.
- For KPI 3, local language version of the website.
- For KPI 4, understand the needs of local customers in different markets and build a specific portfolio catered to their requirements.
- For KPI 5, automate supply and logistics processes on priority.

Following table shows the summary:

	Define	Measure	Analyze	Improve	Control
KPI1	Reduction in the purchase of recommended products	Current state-8%. To be improved to 10% over next 3 months	Need to understand customer preferences better	Online customer survey with incentives	KPI Monitoring over 3 months
KPI2	Less number of new customers visiting the website	Current state-20. To be improved to 25 next month	Insufficient promotions	Additional budget for promotions	
KPI3	Less percentage of new customers making a purchase	Current state-25%. To be improved to 50% over next 3 months	Lack of local language version of website	Local language version of website	
KPI4	Less percentage of revenue increase	Current state-20%. To be improved to 25% over next 3 months	Lack of product portfolio catering to the needs of local customers	Build a portfolio as per local needs	
KPI5	Less percentage of cost reductions	Current state-25%. To be improved to 35% over next 3 months	Lack of automation of supply and logistics processes	Automate on priority	

Group Activity

You can use the following sheet for your KPI review/governance meetings.

KPIs showing amber or red/off-track status	Define	Measure	Analyze	Improve	Control
1.					
2.					
n.					

Summary

- The Transformation types are Core business transformation, Support function transformation and Industry reinvention transformation.

- The popular business models are Platform based, Ad-supported, Freemium, Subscription based, and Access over ownership.
- The Ecosystem selection criteria are Objective, Differentiation, Trust, Governance, and Flexibility.
- The Identification of Change Areas should be as per the Strategic Priorities.
- The Change Areas should be mapped to at least one Digital Technology.
- A Business Case comprises Value and Cost of change. The three types of values are Increased Revenue, Cost Reduction, and Improved Customer Experience.
- There should be at least one Metric or KPI mapped to a Strategic Priority.
- Delivery phase comprises Dashboard Monitoring and Continuous Improvement. They should occur simultaneously.
- The DMAIC continuous improvement method comprises: Define, Measure, Analyze, Improve, Control.

CHAPTER 5

Digital Transformation

You must have heard the buzzword "Digital Transformation" several times. At your workplace, at events and seminars, during coffee breaks with colleagues or causal meetings with friends. Everyone talks about digital transformation. However, not many can understand what it means or how to apply it at their workplaces. There are many definitions and connotations to digital transformation. Some say it is a business transformation. Some call it a cultural transformation. Some say it's about redefining processes. Others call it a technological innovation. *What is it?*

Digital Transformation is the new way of doing business with the help of the latest Digital Technologies.

The new way of doing business implies driving changes in:

- Customer Engagement
- Internal Operations
- Corporate Culture

Customer Engagement is how we interact with and manage relationships with our customers. *Internal Operations* are the daily activities we need to do to keep our business running. *Corporate Culture* refers to values, beliefs, and behaviors that determine how a company's employees and management interact, perform, and handle business transactions.[1]

Digital Technologies include AI, Automation, Cloud, 5G, IoT, Blockchain, Data Science and Data Analytics, Gamification, Virtual/Augmented/Extended-Reality, Metaverse, and so on.

If you just change the way you do business without using any of the digital technologies, it is not Digital Transformation. Or, if you just adopt the digital technologies but stick to your old ways of doing business, it is still not Digital Transformation. Digital Transformation means business transformation using digital technologies. It has a business and a technology component to it.

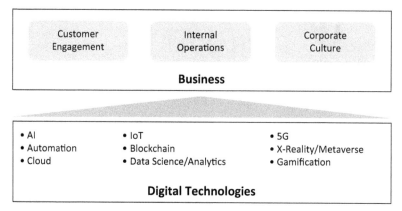

Figure 5.1 Digital Transformation

In almost all industries, Digital Transformation has changed the rules of the game. In the Media industry, TV was the popular medium of content consumption. The old rules of the game were:

- Linearity
- Single screen
- Location bound

All the TV programs were watched linearly. There was no provision for stopping or rewinding a favorite moment. Television was the only screen. There were hardly any alternate devices available. Users had to be bound to a location near the television set to watch their favorite program. However, the new rules of content consumption in the media industry are:

- Linearity + nonlinearity
- Multiscreen
- Mobile

Content can be watched either in a linear or a nonlinear way or on-demand. It can be consumed on multiple screens such as TV, mobile, laptop, desktop, and tablet with mobility anywhere, anytime.

In the Education industry, the old rules of the game were that education had to be:

- Classroom-based
- Uni-directional
- Confined

It was delivered in a classroom flowing unidirectionally from faculty to students. Also, the education was confined to a specific institution. For example, education at MIT or Harvard would be confined only to their respective students. An outsider would not have access to it. However, the new rules of the education industry are:

- Classroom + online
- Collaborative
- Open

Nowadays, education is either classroom-based, online, or a blend of both. It is no longer unidirectional. It is more collaborative: between faculty and students, between faculties, and between students. Education that was once confined to students enrolled at universities only has become open to all. Anyone can have access to any specific courses from top universities through platforms such as edX and Coursera. There are also platforms such as Udemy, where practically anyone can create courses and deliver them to anyone across the globe.

In the Automotive industry, the old rules of the game were that vehicles were:

- Standalone
- Manned
- Fuel-based

But now the vehicles are trending toward becoming ecosystem-supported, autonomous, and electric. In a standalone vehicle, if there is a fault, the driver needs to take it to the technician to get it removed. Whereas in an ecosystem-supported vehicle, all the OEM, spare part manufacturers, and service agents are connected. So, if there is a fault, the fault detection and prevention systems in a vehicle would detect it proactively and offer recommendations to the driver about the nearest technicians and their servicing prices. Currently, vehicles are progressing toward semi-autonomous, a combination of manned and unmanned driving. And finally, there is a transition from fuel-based to more eco-friendly electric vehicles.

Digital technologies have changed the way customers search for information, buy products and services, and communicate with each other. Traditionally, companies relied on surveys, interviews, transaction records, and focus groups to acquire feedback from customers. But now firms can directly seek information on how customers review their products. The digital media plays an important role here. Digital media uses the Internet and mobile to market new products to their customers whereas traditional media uses mainly print, radio, and TV.

Digital media is divided into three categories:

- Paid media
- Owned media
- Earned media

An example of Paid media is the advertisements that pop up while watching YouTube videos. An example of Owned media is the content on the company's website, e-mail subscriptions, newsletters, feeds, alerts, blogs, etc. Earned media are the views, likes, shares, or comments by the users on the company's social media posts.

Over the last decade, a company's marketing budget spending on digital media has grown rapidly than the traditional media. As of February 2022, digital marketing spending increased by 16.2 percent, while traditional grew by 2.9 percent.[2] Ad spending in the digital advertising market worldwide is projected to reach $679.80 billion in 2023.[3] Firms need to be aware of the importance of digital media and understand how to use digital channels to communicate, engage, and influence customers effectively along with traditional media.

DBS, a banking incumbent founded in 1968 as the Development Bank of Singapore, recognized the disruption threats from FinTech companies, emerging due to the changing landscape of the banking sector. There were new financial products in the market, for example, the Alipay payments app from Ant Financials, that were changing the competition landscape dynamically.[4] A survey in the United States showed that 71 percent of millennials would rather go to a dentist than their local bank branch, and three in four preferred financial services from the likes of Google and Amazon.[5] People normally go to banks to fulfill a purpose such as buying a home or a car. They don't come for mortgages and auto loans, and are not interested in the complex paperwork that comes along with these services. Piyush Gupta, the CEO and Director of DBS, strongly felt that there should be a Digital Transformation at DBS. And it needs to happen faster and quicker than its competitors.

With an ambition to become the best digital and people-friendly bank in the world, DBS launched a digital transformation vision— "Making Banking Joyful"[6] with a rebranding tagline "Live More, Bank Less."[7]

To implement the strategy, there were three key strategic initiatives:

1. Embed in customer journey
2. Digital to the core
3. 30,000 startup culture

The first one involved making banking practically "invisible" to the customers and connecting with them more at a personal level. The second one involved making changes to the core of the bank's systems and processes using the latest digital technology. The third one meant creating a startup culture of learning, experimentation, and innovation with a workforce of 30,000.[8]

Customer Engagement

In any business, customer engagement is an important activity as it directly impacts its success. It involves two stages:

1. Digitally connect with customers
2. Digitally interact with customers

We shall discuss digitally connecting with customers through:

1. Paid media
2. Owned media

and digitally interacting with them through:

1. Earned media
2. Chatbots
3. Metaverse

1. Digitally connect through Paid media

A firm can digitally connect with its customers through two types of Paid media: *Search ads* and *Display ads*. Search ads use the concept of pull marketing, whereas display ads use push marketing. Users viewing search ads are already looking for a product or information on the web. Whereas display ads appear to users when they visit a certain web page or watch a video.

Whenever a customer makes a search using certain keywords on the Internet, search engine pops up search ads in the form of sponsored or paid links, location-based ads, or video ads. For example, a keyword search "hotels New York" on Google on a particular day, at a particular time, returns certain sponsored links, and a couple of location-based ads appear at the top left of the search results page, above the organic links. Unlike search ads, display ads do not appear on the search engine results page. They appear on specific websites that are relevant to their own brands that a customer might be interested in. For example, Bank of America may advertise its credit card offers on the *Wall Street Journal* website.

To be visible at the top of the search engine results page, the firms must sign up for search ad campaigns with different search engines.

It is also known as Search Engine Marketing (SEM). Search ad campaigns have three components:

- Goal
- Keywords
- Metrics

Goal of the campaign is based on a firm's objective. It could be increased sales or increased brand awareness. A firm purchases various sets of *Keywords* that are most likely used by a customer while searching for a product or service on the search engine. The keyword sets may differ depending on different geographies and different regional languages. A bid is then placed on each keyword selected, which varies for different keywords. For the keywords that attract higher traffic, the purchase price is higher. The following *Metrics* are used to measure the effectiveness of ad campaigns:

a. Impressions—It is the number of times a search ad is viewed by the users. For example, if a user views a single ad five times a day, it is counted as five impressions.
b. Clicks per Impression—It is the number of clicks an ad impression receives.
c. Click-through rate (CTR)—Clicks divided by the impressions give the click-through rate.
d. Conversion rate—The percentage of clicks that lead to the fulfillment of a campaign objective (sales in most cases).
e. Cost per click (CPC)—The amount spent on search ads divided by the clicks gives cost per click.

Suppose a firm spends $50,000 for search ads with the objective of selling its products. It receives 1 million impressions, 40,000 clicks, and completes 500 sales with a revenue of $150 per sale. Then,

Click-through rate is 4 percent (40,000/1,000,000 × 100)

Conversion rate is 1.25 percent (500/40,000 × 100)

Cost per click is $1.25 (50,000/40,000) and

Search ad profit is $25,000 (($500 \times 150) - 50,000$)

The positioning of search ads on the search results page plays an important role. Eye-tracking studies show that users focus on the top region of the search engine results page more. As they move down the page the attention diminishes. The top region is called the Golden Triangle for search engine results. All the companies want the ad to be displayed in the Golden Triangle. However, the positioning of a search ad depends on two factors:

- Quality Score
- Cost per Click bid

Quality score is determined by how relevant the ad is to the customer which is measured by the click-through rate and the quality of the landing page which is measured by a metric called Bounce rate. *Bounce rate* is determined by how quickly the customers leave the page after landing. *Cost per click bid* is the amount a firm bids on a specific selected keyword which depends on search ad budget, competition, expected click-through rate, and the expected conversion rate.

For search ads, a few top search engines such as Google, Yahoo, Microsoft Bing dominate the value chain. But for the display ad industry, there are different players in the value chain as shown in Figure 5.2. Display ads could be text ads, image ads, or video ads.

Advertisers are the buyers who buy online space for ads to reach their target customers. *Publishers* are the sellers who sell online space to advertisers. *Ad Networks* aggregate the supply of advertising space from

Figure 5.2 Display ad value chain

various publishers and match it with the advertiser's demand. They also develop proprietary algorithms to help advertisers strategically place ads on various websites.[9] *Ad exchanges* orchestrate matching between advertisers and publishers using a real-time auction process. They are like stock exchanges that match stock buyers and sellers. *Demand Side Platforms or DSPs* help manage the ad inventory across multiple Ad Exchanges. *Supply Side Platforms or SSPs* help publishers get the best prices for their ad space inventory from various buyers. The SSPs and DSPs are like stockbrokers.

The following metrics are used to measure the display ad effectiveness:

a. Cost per thousand impressions (CPM)
b. Cost per click (CPC)
c. Cost per view (CPV) (video ads)

Suppose a firm spends $50,000 with the objective of selling its products. It receives 10 million impressions, 40,000 clicks, and completes 500 sales with a revenue of $150 per sale.

Then,

Click-through rate is 0.4 percent (40,000/10,000,000 × 100)

Conversion rate is 1.25 percent (500/40,000 × 100)

Cost per thousand impressions is $5 (50,000/10,000,000 × 1000)

Display ad profit is $25,000 ((500 × 150) − 50,000)

2. Digitally connect through Owned media

Digitally connecting with customers through Owned media includes connecting through websites, blogs, podcasts, white papers, etc. The customers type the keywords in the search engine related to a company's product or service. Several organic links are displayed below the sponsored links in the search results. If a firm wants more traffic on its business links, they should be displayed higher in the organic search results, perhaps on the first page. This is known as Search Engine Optimization or SEO. It is the process of improving the quality and quantity of web traffic to a website or webpage from search engines.[10]

The organic links are displayed on the search results page in a specific order. We saw from the Golden Triangle principle that customers do not look beyond the top few organic links on the first page of the search results. The companies need to find ways to achieve higher rankings in search engines. SEO works on two factors:

- Relevance
- Authority

Relevance is the measure of how closely a search engine can match the customer search query and a particular web page. This is based on page title, page content, and meta tags which are the lines of code in the header section of a web page containing information about its structure. *Authority* of a web page is based on the number and authority of other web pages it is linked to.[11] Thus, a company, for a successful SEO must ensure the following three things:

First, its website has the content, keywords, and meta tags to improve its relevance to a particular search query to rank it higher in the organic search results.

Second, make sure that there are quality inbound links from other websites.

And third, deciding what content on the landing page should appear once the customer clicks an organic link.

3. Digitally interact through Earned media

Earned media or social media is a powerful tool that allows people to share information and ideas across the globe. Intuit co-founder Scott Cook stated its importance, "A brand is no longer what we tell the customer it is. It is what the customers tell each other." Firms can use the earned media to digitally interact with the customer in two ways:

First, understand the customer. How do customers perceive our brand? What do they like or dislike? How do they associate with the brand?[12]

Second, participate in social conversations that create opportunities for real-time marketing.

For example, Starbucks launched the open innovation platform "My Starbucks Idea" to source new ideas from the customers on how their preferred Starbucks should look. Over the first five years of operations, Starbucks received over 150,000 ideas and implemented over hundreds of them.[13] The customers had to create a user profile on the platform and submit their ideas for others to comment on. The ideas that received the maximum votes from people were displayed on a public leaderboard, with the picture of the idea creator next to it. Thus, the customers felt their voices heard, which increased their brand loyalty.

4. Digitally interact through Chatbots

Chatbots are virtual users that simulate a conversation with another human. Most of the bots existing today are application-specific and are developed by a human coder. A simple chatbot contains a code based on simple if-then statements. A more sophisticated chatbot would use Artificial Intelligence (AI), Machine Learning, and Deep Learning technologies offering a customized experience to its customers. As per an analyst report, the global chatbot market is expected worth $15.5 billion by 2028, growing at a CAGR of 23.3 percent.[14]

The following table shows the applications of bots.

Areas	Value bots can provide
Customer Service	Handle customer service requests, offer alerts and information, manage account settings and preferences, and communicate in multiple languages
Commerce	Place orders, process payments, handle shipping preferences, and respond to questions
Sales and Marketing	Deliver campaigns and offers, make recommendations, offer loyalty incentives, and deliver relevant content
Recruitment	Interact with candidates, answer questions, and schedule meetings
Healthcare	Offer medicine reminders, health and safety alerts, communicate with physicians, and manage resource inventory
Government	Manage visa applications, solve basic tax-related queries, and resolve parking tickets
Smart home devices	Control heating, manage security, control home appliances, control and automate devices
Transportation	Retrieve information about traffic conditions, remotely lock vehicles, and call ride-share services
Employee Productivity	Manage calendar, e-mail, search, and plan daily tasks
Personal Finance	Manage by receiving alerts, checking balances, processing transfers and payments

With advanced Machine Learning and Deep Learning algorithms, bots can do a lot more.

In November 2022, OpenAI launched ChatGPT, an AI-based chatbot, that allows one to have human-like conversations with the machine and can supposedly provide answers to any questions you type in the chat box. The GPT stands for Generative Pretrained Transformer. As the name says, it is a generative AI, which means it generates a new answer (content) in the form of different images, text, audio, and so on. Some Generative AI applications use a type of deep learning called Generative Adversarial Networks (GANs) to create new content. A GAN consists of two neural networks: a generator that creates new data and a discriminator that evaluates the data. The generator and discriminator work together, with the generator improving its outputs based on the feedback it receives from the discriminator until it generates content that is indistinguishable from real data.[15] The generative AI is based on huge foundation models. The foundation model used by ChatGPT is GPT-3.5. It has over 175 billion parameters[16] trained over 499 billion words, and harvested over millions of websites. The business applications of ChatGPT could be enhancing customer engagement, automating customer support, and improving customer experience.

5. Digitally interact through Metaverse

Currently, there are lots of ongoing discussions around how to interact with customers on Metaverse. Businesses can create virtual stores or office spaces in the Metaverse. Customers using their avatars can visit these virtual stores. As they enter the store, they would be greeted by the store attendant's avatar. There should be a real person operating behind the avatar. Through avatars, the customers and the store attendant can communicate in real-time using the microphone and the headsets over the metaverse. The customers can shop for various products in the virtual store and the attendant can guide them through the purchasing process. Once a final selection of a product is made, the customer should be guided to a checkout counter. There could be two payment options: payment through the metaverse or payment through the real world, depending upon the customer's preference. More details on metaverse will be covered in Appendix: Digital Technologies.

Let us understand how customer engagement was managed at DBS. The tagline—"Live More, Bank Less" for the Digital Transformation vision—"Making Banking Joyful" meant making it easier for customers to conduct their banking by leveraging digital technologies.

To implement the strategic initiative, embed in customer journey, DBS used the 4D framework: Discover, Define, Develop, and Deploy. Piyush first started with an off-site retreat with his senior management team of 250 people and board members, where two days were spent training them on customer journey mapping. Lots of time was spent on the "Discover" part of the framework, where intense focus was not only on the physical aspect of what the customer does but also on the emotional motives that drive a certain behavior of the customer. DBS observed the customer interactions happening on the digital platforms to get a better understanding of customer journeys in the digital world. DBS calls it "Customer Science." It began tracking down every single detail of the customer behavior; what are their pain points, where do they get stuck, where do they fall off?[17]

One of the key challenges of embedding in the customer journeys was to convert the current traditional customers into digital and to convince them to transact with the bank digitally. DBS came up with three behavioral criteria for the digital customers:

1. Product purchase or segment upgrade via digital channels OR
2. More than 50 percent of financial transactions via digital channels OR
3. More than 50 percent of nonfinancial transactions via digital channels. The customers had to re-qualify on a rolling 12-month basis.[18]

To better engage with customers digitally, DBS launched:

1. "Sparks," an industry-first online mini-web series inspired by true client and employee stories, depicting how a group of young bankers challenge the status quo and go above and beyond when solving unusual client challenges.[19] Since its inception, Sparks garnered 245 million views as well as more than 24 million engagements globally.[20]
2. "DBS PayLah!," a mobile app for making cashless payments, getting rides, booking shows, ordering food, requesting funds from friends, and viewing e-statements within the app.[21]

3. iWealth, a faster, smarter, and more personalized way to give greater control of wealth and better access to investment opportunities.[22]

4. Treasury Prism, the world's first online treasury and cash management simulation platform for CFOs and corporate treasurers.[23]

5. DBS Marketplace, a one-stop portal to browse property listings, cars, book travel, flights, hotels, and compare utility providers.[24]

Internal Operations

As shown in Figure 5.3, the Internal Operations consist of Delivery Operations and Sales Operations.

Delivery Operations consist of Product or Service Delivery, Finance, Supply and Logistics, and Sourcing and Partnering. They include four major customer touch points:

- Delivery
- Acceptance
- Invoice
- Payment

Sales Operations consist of all the operations related to sales and marketing and includes four major touch points:

- Lead
- Opportunity
- Contract
- Order

The Internal Operations comprise various processes between different functions causing data flow between them. These processes can be optimized using digital technologies such as AI, Automation, Data Science, and Analytics, which can help in reducing costs. How these technologies impact Internal Operations is explained in detail in Appendix: Digital Technologies.

Let us understand how Internal Operations were managed at DBS. DBS had an ambition to transform its Internal Operations to be more like

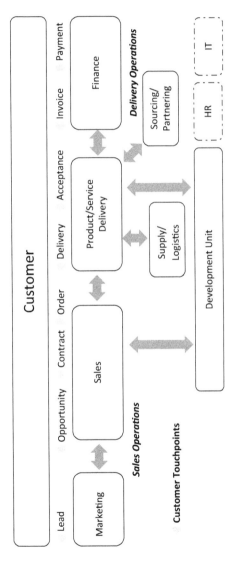

Figure 5.3 Internal Operations

a technical company than a financial or banking institute. Dave Gledhill, the CTO of DBS coined the acronym "GANDALF." The first letters of Google, Amazon, Netflix, DBS, Apple, LinkedIn, and Facebook together spelled GANDALF.

"Let's be the D in GANDALF." said Dave.

The plan for DBS was to use open-source software like Google, run on cloud platforms like Amazon, use data and automation to scale, provide personalized recommendations like Netflix, design like Apple, be a learning community and push for continuous learning like LinkedIn, and become more collective like Facebook.[25]

Dave said:

We said to our people, 'Don't compare yourself to other banks. Compare yourself to technology companies because that's now the benchmarking we're operating against.' And it had this great cultural effect of setting people free to be bold enough to really drive change and not be constrained by the way banks normally do things.

To implement GANDALF, five key pillars were identified:

1. Shift from products to platform
2. Organize for success
3. Develop high-performing agile teams
4. Automate everything
5. Design for modern systems[26]

To achieve the above objectives, DBS got rid of bureaucracy, discarded steering committees, and eliminated multiple approvals at every stage. This reduced the lead times and added speed and efficiency to the processes. Teams were reorganized with technical and business teams being integrated into one, which shared common goals and visions. DevOps methodology was adopted along with automation to develop new platforms and solutions in a Continuous Integration Continuous Deployment (CI/CD) format. Most of the technology services that were outsourced to vendor firms were insourced. There was a focus on developing technical competencies in-house and people with technical skills were hired. Most of the technical applications and platforms were moved to the cloud.[27]

In 2017, DBS launched the developer platform of APIs, to bring together partners from various industries in an ecosystem. Currently, the platform has more than 1000 open APIs. For instance, cars can now be bought and sold on the bank's platform, with DBS car loans integrated seamlessly into the system. Thus, DBS becomes "invisible" to its customers while meeting their needs.[28]

Corporate Culture

To enable Digital Transformation, the incumbents must embrace the culture of learning and innovation. They must facilitate the employees to cultivate a digital mindset that encourages experimentation and rethink the way people work together. However, a big challenge that every firm faces is getting everyone in the organization inspired and motivated to embrace a culture of change and innovation. Current Gallup data shows a startling statistic that only 15 percent of employees worldwide are engaged at work. This means that the majority of the workforce around the world is either viewing their workplace negatively or only doing the bare minimum to make it through the day, with little to no emotional attachment.[29] Hence, it is very important for many organizations, that a cultural transformation happens first before a digital transformation. To enable a cultural transformation, it is important to understand the types of employees and what motivates them. There are five types of people at work:

- Type 1
- Type 2
- Type 3
- Type 4
- Type 5

For Type 1, work is never a priority. They can be valuable employees often dependable and hardworking, but their focus is elsewhere, on their family or hobbies or some creative pursuits. These are the staff you will find mainly in administrative or in the back office. They often work hard because their work provides them with security in their personal life.

Type 2 care deeply about the social purpose of work, which is changing the world. They think, are we building something that will last? Programers, technologists, architects, and engineers are the ones who belong to such category.

Type 3 are motivated by a sense of stability and progress and flourish when companies offer them a clear plan to develop and grow over time.

Type 4 are team-oriented, motivated by collaboration with others.

Type 5 are the risk takers that want to know they are pushing it to the limits. They recognize they could lose big, but they are attracted to the idea that they could win big. Type 2 or the "world changers" and Type 5 or the "risk takers" are the best types of people for enabling cultural transformation. The best way to motivate these categories is to offer them autonomy and recognition.[30]

To implement a start-up culture among 30,000 DBS employees, DBS introduced a program "Culture by Design," which was defined by the acronym ABCDE[31]:

- Agile
- Be a learning organization
- Customer obsessed
- Data-driven
- Experiment and take risks

Agile methodology was implemented by reducing the lead time of the processes, removing the layers of bureaucracy and approvals, and making meetings effective and productive with bank-wide meeting best practice known as "Meeting MoJo." Mo stands for Meeting Owner and Jo stands for Joyful Observer.[32] The Meeting Owner ensures everyone has an equal share of voice, while Joyful Observer ensures that the meeting is on time, sticks to the agenda, and provides feedback to Mo at the end.[33] MoJo produced serious benefits helping the bank save more than 500,000 employee hours.[34]

Being a learning organization involved building a growth mindset among its employees so that they could continuously learn, grow, and adapt.[35]

Customer obsession involved everyday operations and efforts to resolve challenges by thinking about the "job to be done" for the customers and implementation of customer journeys to find new solutions.[36]

Data-driven involves establishing robust data governance capabilities and practices across five core dimensions: data access and security, data ownership, data understanding, data quality, and responsible data use. DBS has also implemented its PURE Framework to ensure responsible data use across the bank, with data use cases assessed against the PURE Principles (Purposeful, Unsurprising, Respectful, Explainable). This has been further enabled through the development of an in-house assessment tool overlaid with formal governance procedures, operating models, and the introduction of mandatory training.[37]

To implement experiments and take risks, DBS organized five-day hackathons to bring out change and innovations. It created a "DBS Daredevil Award" to recognize staff who had dared to try and experiment without the fear of failing.[38]

"Making Banking Joyful" initiative became a top priority for the top executives at DBS. KPIs were introduced and monitored in real time using dashboards. In total, 20 percent of the balanced scorecard was allocated to "Making Banking Joyful," 40 percent to traditional KPIs, and 40 percent to strategic priorities. The "Making Banking Joyful" Digital Transformation KPIs were divided into four categories: Ecosystem, Acquire, Transact, and Engage.[39]

Results of Digital Transformation at DBS[40]

- DBS expanded in 18 markets across the globe, with Singapore, Hong Kong, Taiwan, Indonesia, India, and China, being the priority.
- In 2015 and 2016, the audit team won the Institution of Engineers Singapore's engineering awards for its innovation in technology and use of data analytics in predictive risk identification.
- Digital customers brought twice the income and had grown from 33 percent of the base in 2015 to 48 percent in 2018.

- In 2018, DBS won Global Finance's "Best Bank in the World" and Euromoney's "Best Digital Bank in the World" awards.
- At the beginning of 2019, with 10 million retail customers and over 200,000 institutional customers, it made $4.13 billion in profits and $9.68 billion in net sales.
- Then in 2019, it became the first bank in the world to be awarded the best bank in the world award concurrently for Euromoney, Global Finance, and The Banker, as well as receiving several other accolades.

Summary

- Digital Transformation has a business and a technology component.
- Business areas include Customer Engagement, Internal Operations, and Corporate Culture.
- Digital technologies include AI, Automation, Data Science and Analytics, Cloud, Blockchain, 5G, IoT, Gamification, Extended Reality, and Metaverse.
- Customer Engagements include:
  1. Digitally connecting with customers
  2. Digitally interacting with customers
- Digitally connecting includes connecting with customers through Paid and Owned media.
- Digitally interacting includes interacting with customers through Earned media, Chatbots, and Metaverse.

CHAPTER 6

Talent XYZ–A Fictitious Case Study

It was a cold and gloomy day in December. The temperature had dropped to below freezing. It had just begun to snow. The snowflakes trickled down the streets of Gamla Stan, the famous old town of Stockholm. Roads became icy and slippery. Soon layers of snow began to accumulate. Everything turned white. The whole landscape was transformed. Gazing at this beautiful change in the surroundings through his office window, Nils Sjoblom, the founder and CEO of Talent XYZ, a Stockholm-based Human Resource Management (HRM) software company, began to ponder while sipping on his favorite cappuccino, how could he digitally transform the company.

Two quarters ago, to stay at par with the competition, Talent XYZ ran a pilot on Robotic Process Automation, where an attempt was made to automate the manual, administrative, and repetitive processes in operations through bots, to cut down the operational costs. The problem was that any change in the IT environment such as a URL change would stop the bots from functioning. A support team had to be deployed to troubleshoot them, which made their maintenance expensive. It was not a scalable business case. The pilot had failed.

Times were critical for Talent XYZ. Sales were on the decline. The software industry was transforming. The customers were looking for something new and different. There was a dearth of digital competence in the firm. There were constant disruption threats from digital attackers. There was a severe pressure from the board.

Digital Transformation was inevitable!

Nils knew that many things at Talent XYZ needed to change. But he had no clue where to begin from. The more he thought, the more he became lost and confused. He had several meetings and workshops with his leadership team. There were lots of discussions. New ideas came up. But most of them were conflicting with one another. No one really stood up to take ownership and drive change. Things did not move anywhere. Talent XYZ needed an external help very badly.

Last week, Nils was involved in a day-long brainstorming workshop with his leadership team to finalize the external vendor to consult and advise Talent XYZ on Digital Transformation. Three firms were shortlisted:

1. Dunham & Mercer Consulting Group, New York City, 10k employees, offices in over 10 countries.
2. Prudential & Co, London, 200k employees, offices in over 50 countries.
3. Holm Advisory Services, Oslo, 5k employees, offices mainly in Scandinavia.

His leadership team presented their views on the vendor selection. But Nils had to make the final decision that would decide the future of Talent XYZ, with 2500 employees and offices in 12 countries across the globe, serving some of the top EU-originated global brands over two decades. Which one would he select?

While Nils was absorbed in a deep thought, glancing at the evening snow, an e-mail popped up in his inbox, making the notable Microsoft 365 Outlook sound to announce its arrival. It was from an unknown external sender. It read:

Dear Nils,

Hope you are doing fine!

I am the founder of Digiculum, a Stockholm-based firm offering Digital Transformation services such as Consulting, Learning, and Ecosystem Orchestration, for some of the top European clients.

First step toward successful digital transformation is a Digital Strategy. Unlike other consultants, we differentiate ourselves by helping you create and execute a digital strategy for your organization through our unique and proprietary strategy framework.

We believe that Learning is not just a one-time but a continuous process. We help our clients apply skills and concepts learnt in the classroom to real business environments.

We onboard our clients onto an ecosystem, where people collaborate to share best practices, ways of working, success stories, and experiences. We currently orchestrate an ecosystem in the Nordics, comprising some of the top global brands.

We would love to be your transformation partners. Could we have a brief online or a face-to-face meeting to discuss more?

Yours truly,
Sarah Stilwell
Founder and CEO
Digiculum

There were hundreds of mass promotion e-mails received by the company every day. IT had turned on strict spam filters to screen out the suspected spam and junk e-mails from unknown external senders. But somehow this e-mail managed to journey through the filters and land in Nils's mailbox. He liked the content of the e-mail as it addressed Talent XYZ's need of the hour. He was very curious to know more about Digiculum's strategy framework and ecosystem orchestration. However, he had already been through a painstaking process of shortlisting external vendors for transformation with his leadership team and didn't want a new one.

Nils gave another look at the e-mail. He saw the Digiculum's office address on the e-mail signature. It read "Futura, Stockholm."

He smiled.

Before incubating Talent XYZ in 2003 in Stockholm, Sweden, Nils was the Head of Talent Acquisition at T&S Group, one of the top global Nordic fashion brands. It was his first job after graduation and worked there for 14 years. His work involved recruiting the best talents. At T&S, most of the HRM processes were done manually through Excel and the talent management software used was not efficient. It did not provide unified workflows for fundamental processes of HRM. This was the issue with not only T&S but with the entire HRM software industry. He saw an opportunity and decided to start his own venture. He left T&S at age 35 and formed a company named Talent XYZ. The main motive behind the name was that he wanted to build a brand that catered to managing talents across all the industries for all the generations—X, Y, and Z.

Talent XYZ was a bootstrap or a self-funded venture. Nils had invested most of his savings from his job into his own company. He rented a small desk at a co-working space named Futura, in the Stockholm city center near T-Centralen. It was shared by different startups. The ambience at Futura was phenomenal with creative and futuristic interiors. The place was filled with high energy and ambitions; people pouring in and out, daily seminars and events, and a cozy cafe that sold one of the finest coffees to stimulate entrepreneurs at work. Just the right kind of environment needed for Nils to overcome the feeling of quitting his new venture.

Nils interviewed different key people in HR from various industries to understand their needs and pain points. After making a thorough analysis of the situation, he decided to develop his own HRM tool. It took 10 months for the first version of the product to be developed and ready to go to the market. Nils had been working on the sales strategy while the product development was going on in parallel. His focus was the B2B customers, comprising small and mid-sized organizations. One of his former colleagues at T&S helped him acquire his first customer. Thereafter, over the next two decades, Talent XYZ grew and became a multimillion euro enterprise, serving different clients across different industries.

The organization chart of Talent XYZ is shown in Figure 6.1. There are two main business units: Software and Services. The business unit Software is divided into Product Development and Presales Support Software units. Product Development unit comprises Design and Testing. The Design team continuously develops new versions and new features of the products, while the Testing team tests them to ensure they meet the customer requirements. Presales Support Software team comprises the technical subject matter experts who support the sales team in selling products to the customers.

The business unit Services is divided into three units: Integration, Maintenance and Support, and Presales Support Services. The Integration team is further divided into Install and Configure. The Install team does

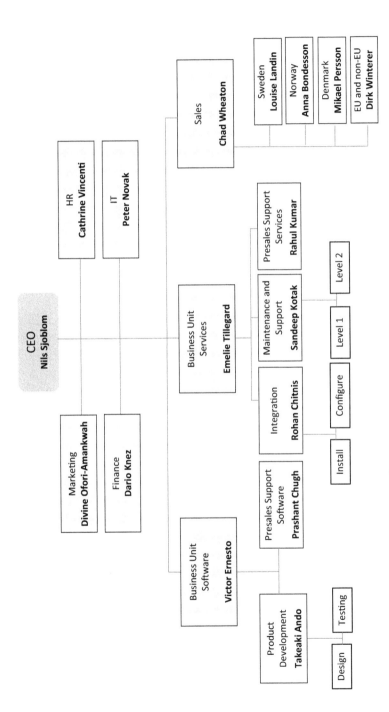

Figure 6.1 Talent XYZ organization chart

the installation of HRM software and the Configure team makes it go live into the customer's IT environment. The Maintenance and Support team provides 24 × 7 support to the customers by troubleshooting the issues related to the software. This unit is further divided into Level 1 and Level 2 support. The Level 1 support team is the first point of escalation in case of any customer issues. Those that are not resolved by Level 1 are escalated to Level 2 team further. Presales Support Services unit comprises consultants, working closely with the Presales Support Software and supporting the sales teams in selling products to the customers.

The Sales unit is divided into four accounts: Sweden, Norway, Denmark, and EU and non-EU, serving customers located in those specific markets. At the bottom of the chart, we find employees in each of these teams reporting to a line manager. Also supporting the business, we have Finance, Marketing, IT, and HR units.

Nils Sjoblom's leadership team (L1) included:

- Victor Ernesto, Head of Business Unit Software
- Emelie Tillegard, Head of Business Unit Services
- Chad Wheaton, Head of Sales
- Divine Ofori-Amankwah, Head of Marketing
- Dario Knez, Head of Finance
- Peter Novak, Head of IT
- Cathrine Vincenti, Head of HR

Following is the comparison of offers received by Talent XYZ:

Name	Resources	Hourly Rates (EUR)	Man Hours	Offer (EUR)
Dunham & Mercer	7 full-time employees (FTE): 2 Analysts 3 Consultants 1 Project Manager 1 Partner	Analyst: 60 Consultant: 80 Project Manager: 110 Partner: 150	Analyst: 300 Consultant: 300 Project Manager: 100 Partner: 25	56,750
Prudential & Co	6 FTE: 2 Analysts 2 Consultants 1 Project Manager 1 Partner	Analyst: 70 Consultant: 90 Project Manager: 120 Partner: 150	Analyst: 200 Consultant: 200 Project Manager: 200 Partner: 50	63,500

Name	Resources	Hourly Rates (EUR)	Man Hours	Offer (EUR)
Holm Advisory Services	8 FTE: 3 Analysts 3 Consultants 1 Project Manager 1 Partner	Analyst: 80 Consultant: 100 Project Manager: 130 Partner: 150	Analyst: 300 Consultant: 300 Project Manager: 100 Partner: 50	74,500

Nils smiled as he read Futura. It reminded him of his early startup days 20 years ago. The beginnings were humble and Nils cherished every single moment of them.

As he hovered the mouse cursor over the delete button, he changed his mind in a flash and clicked the "Reply" button.

He wrote:

Dear Sarah,

Thank you for reaching out to me. Can you please meet me at my office in Gamla stan, Tuesday next week, at 15:00?

Regards,
Nils

At the meeting, after mutual introductions, Sarah asked "Can you please elaborate more on the end-to-end HR processes?"

Nils replied:

HRM is a very important function of every organization. It involves end-to-end activities such as hiring, onboarding, developing, appraising, compensating, retaining, and exiting.

The objective of hiring is to find a person whose skills, abilities, and personal characteristics suit the job. It is a question of fit between the individual and the requirements of the position.

Once hiring is done, the next step is onboarding. A new hire is mostly excited and motivated to start a new position at a company and it is the duty of the HR to make the 'Day one' experience a memorable one.

Employees need to be continuously developed on the job which includes training, motivating, coaching, and mentoring at every step. There are three types of training delivery methods: On-the-job training or OJT, Collaboration, Classroom-based or Online training. In OJT, a candidate is deployed on a new role or assignment and given an opportunity to learn and develop new skills. Collaboration involves learning in a group or knowledge sharing with other colleagues while doing the daily job. Most employees prefer a blend of classroom and online training.

There are two types of Motivation: Extrinsic and Intrinsic. Researchers at Harvard Business School have developed a model of motivation that establishes a link between motivation, employee productivity, and company profitability. Customer loyalty drives profitability. Customer satisfaction drives customer loyalty. Values drive customer satisfaction. Employee productivity drives values. Employee loyalty drives employee productivity. Employee satisfaction drives employee loyalty. And motivation drives employee satisfaction.

Coaching at workplace is one of the most powerful tools for developing people. When employees are under pressure to produce results, they get stressed. Stress can also be due to other reasons such as insufficient support or resources, lack of recognition, conflict of values, or changes in an organization. Stress limits beliefs and behaviors which locks the potential of employees. Coaching helps to change the beliefs and build behaviors that drive employee performance. In coaching, the coach doesn't provide answers but rather enables the employee to come up with his/her solutions to problems.

Mentoring is a relationship between two people with the goal of professional and personal development. The "mentor" is usually an experienced individual who shares knowledge, experience, and advice with a "mentee" who is less experienced. Mentors support and encourage their mentees by offering suggestions and knowledge to improve their skills and advance their careers. A mentoring partnership may be between two people within the same company, same industry, or different industries.

Performance appraisal is a formal method of assessing how well an individual employee is doing with respect to assigned goals. Its ultimate purpose is to communicate personal goals, motivate good performance, provide constructive feedback, and set the stage for an effective development plan.

Employees tend to quit if their needs are not met by a firm. Whenever an employee leaves, a company loses its knowledge and often expensively acquired skills. And whenever that employee goes to the competitor, the loss is compounded as your competitors gain its knowledge base without having to invest the time and money in training your company may have invested.

The exit should be managed smoothly as an employee leaving the organization on a good note will be its promoter. There should be an alumni network developed and managed by HR. It is much easier and less expensive to re-hire alumni. Also, there are more chances of acquiring new sales for an organization through its alumni networks.

"What is your digital strategy?" asked Sarah.

"We want to digitalize our products and services for the customer." said Nils.

"That's your mission statement and not your strategy." said Sarah. "To enable digital transformation, the first important thing is to have a Digital Strategy. Through our Digital Strategy Framework, we can help you create and execute a Digital Strategy."

"That seems impressive!" said Nils. "How much is your offer?"

We would like to offer you advisory services on Digital Strategy only. There will be a team of four, three consultants and myself. Total man-hours would be 80 and we charge 150 euros per hour. So, the total offer is EUR 12,000.

said Sarah.

Nils couldn't believe his ears. The price was one-fifth of what the other consultants were offering him. Also, they were jumping right into the Digital Transformation, without taking into consideration the Digital Strategy.

"So, when do we get started?" asked Nils.

"We can get started Monday next week." said Sarah.

I would need your organization chart and the names and e-mails of your L1 and L2 leadership. I will send out the Digital Maturity Assessment to fill in. Then, there would be detailed one-hour interviews with each of them. After that, we should have a two-day workshop with your L1 and L2 leaders.

"Sounds like a plan!" exclaimed Nils.
Nils wrote an e-mail to his leadership team:

Dear All,

I just had a meeting with Sarah Stilwell, the founder of Digiculum, who would guide us through developing a Digital Strategy for Talent XYZ. They have offered us EUR 12,000 for 80 hours and I have accepted the offer. Let's roll it off!

Regards,
Nils

It was Monday 9 am. Sarah began writing an e-mail. In the sender's list, besides Nils and his L1 leadership team, she added the following L2 leaders:

Takeaki Ando-Director Product Development
Prashant Chugh- Director Presales Support Software
Rohan Chitnis-Director Integration
Sandeep Kotak-Director Maintenance and Support
Rahul Kumar-Director Presales Support Services
Louise Landin-KAM Sweden
Anna Bondesson-KAM Norway
Mikael Persson-KAM Denmark
Dirk Winterer-KAM EU and non-EU accounts

The Digital Maturity Assessment questionnaire was included in the e-mail as an attachment with instructions on how to fill it. It had to be returned in the next two days.

After Sarah received all the assessment responses, she calculated the aggregated average score for the company, which was as follows:

New Business Adoption	Your score
Customer Engagement	
1 We clearly understand our customer's business needs	3
2 We translate customer needs into solutions	2
3 We constantly put in perspective how work relates to customer success	1
4 We seek continuous feedback from customers	1
5 We constantly innovate new ways of engaging with customer	1
6 Our sales team is competent with new digital skills	2
7 Customer data is accessible to us in real-time	1
8 Our customer processes are automated	1
9 We receive continuous data on our product/service performance	1
10 We have a culture of customer first	5
11 Our customers trust us as reliable partners	3
12 We offer better experience to our customers	3
13 We have better insights on our customers	2
14 We have efficient systems to track customer behavior	1
a) Average score	1.9
Internal Operations	
15 Our internal business processes are automated	3
16 We monitor our internal operational processes in real-time	1
17 We make decisions based on data analytics	1
18 We use dashboards to monitor the operational KPIs	1
19 Our supplier processes are automated	1
20 We can monitor our supplier data in real-time	1
21 We achieve considerable cost savings through our digitalized operations	2
22 We have integrated financial data and systems	2
23 We have digitalized our HR processes	2
24 We manage our inventories in real-time	1
b) Average score	1.5
Corporate Culture	
25 People have desire to learn new digital skills	2
26 People are willing to invest time and effort in learning	3
27 We have an effective individual learning system	3
28 We innovate continuously	2
29 We often share knowledge and re-use information	3
30 Our leaders exemplify a culture of learning and innovation	3

(Continues)

(*Continued*)

	New Business Adoption	Your score
31	We offer psychological safety to our employees	3
32	We have a strong feedback system	3
33	We have a startup culture	2
34	We orchestrate ecosystems at our workplace	1
35	We have a clear digital transformation strategy	1
c)	Average score	2.4
	Final Score: a + b + c	5.8

	Digital Technology Adoption	Your score
	Data	
1	Our data is available in real-time	1
2	Our data is easily accessible	3
3	Our data flows seamlessly between the systems	2
4	We derive useful insights from our data	1
5	We have efficient data aggregation and curation methods	1
6	We capture data at various touchpoints across our customer journey	3
7	We make data-driven business decisions	1
8	We have rigid data security and integrity measures	2
a)	Average score	1.75
	IT Tools	
9	We understand the business criticality of the tools	3
10	We continuously monitor our tool usage	3
11	We continuously upgrade our tools	5
12	We know the operational costs of all our tools	3
13	Our tools offer data and information security	4
14	Our tools are customizable	3
15	Our tools are reusable	2
16	Our tools integrate well with other tools in our IT environment	4
17	We have a good control over redundant tools	3
18	We use virtual assistants/chatbots for IT support	2
b)	Average score	3.2
	Apps	
19	We have migrated most applications to cloud	2
20	We have a good cloud migration strategy	1

	Digital Technology Adoption		Your score
21	We innovate in cloud		2
c)		Average score	1.6
	Technical Competence		
22	We have strong AI/ML competence		2
23	We have strong Automation competence		2
24	We have strong IoT competence		1
25	We have strong Data Science competence		1
26	We have strong Cloud competence		2
27	We have strong Digital Marketing competence		2
28	We have strong Coding skills		5
29	We have strong Platform Engineering skills		4
30	We have strong IT infrastructure management skills		4
d)		Average score	2.5
	Final Score: a + b + c + d		9.05

For New Business Adoption, the average score for Customer Engagement was 1.9, for Internal Operations was 1.5, and for Corporate Culture was 2.4. The total score was 5.8, corresponding to "LOW." For Digital Technology Adoption, the average score for Data was 1.75, for IT tools was 3.2, for Apps was 1.6, and for Technical Competence was 2.5. The total score for Digital Technology Adoption was 9.05, corresponding to "LOW." As both New Business Adoption and Digital Technology Adoption were "Low," Talent XYZ was at Digital Maturity Level 1.

Sarah e-mailed the scores to Nils. It was a matter of concern for him. She suggested next week Thursday and Friday for a two-day full workshop. Nils was aware of the urgency and told all the L1 and L2 leaders to prioritize this workshop.

A week later, all the workshop participants gathered at an offsite location. After a round of introductions, Sarah projected the final aggregated Digital Maturity Assessment scores for the company. There was silence in the conference room. Then, Sarah began with the Industry Analysis. She divided the 17 participants into 4 groups and handed the Industry Analysis questionnaire to each of them. All of them began to fill in as per the instructions. At the end, the average group scores for each group were calculated. And then the average of each group average score was calculated as the final aggregated company score which was as follows:

		Your Score
	Threat of New Entrants	
1	Upfront capital investments are low	2
2	Cost of switching from one supplier to another is low	4
3	Incumbents don't have a strong power position	3
4	There are a wide range of distribution channels available	5
5	Ease of doing business is high	5
6	Exit costs from industry are low	3
7	Industry growth is rapid	4
a)	Average score	3.7
	Bargaining Power of Suppliers	
8	Suppliers have better control over price	2
9	Suppliers have strong dominance	2
10	Switching costs from one supplier to another are high	3
11	Supplier products are unique or highly differentiated	1
12	There are few or no substitutes available for supplier products	1
13	Supplier offers its products or services to multiple industries	4
b)	Average score	2.1
	Bargaining Power of Buyers	
14	Buyer dominance is high	4
15	Buyer can switch from one supplier product to another with low costs	4
16	There are many undifferentiated products/services available	4
c)	Average score	4
	Availability of Substitutes	
17	There are many available substitutes for product/service	2
18	It is easy to access or acquire substitutes	3
19	Buyers would pay for lower quality substitutes available at lower price	3
d)	Average score	2.6
	Rivalry among Competitors	
20	There are many incumbents in our industry	5
21	Competition on price is intense among the incumbents	6
22	Products are highly undifferentiated	5
23	Switching costs from one incumbent product to another is low	5

		Your Score
24	Industry growth is slow	4
25	Cost of exiting the industry is high	5
26	Incumbents fight to steal market share from one another	5
e)	Average score	5
	Final Score: a + b + c + d + e	17.4

Legend:

between 5 and 10: High Industry Profitability

between 11 and 20: Moderate Industry Profitability

between 21 and 30: Low Industry Profitability

She said to the audience "Your industry shows moderate profitability. I have two questions for you: First, how to increase Talent XYZ's profits? Second, what are the potential threats to existing profits?"

"To increase Talent XYZ's profits, we must increase our product sales." said Chad.

"We need to lower our product development costs." said Takeaki.

"The increased competition in the software market from new digital players is the threat to existing profits." said Emelie.

"Which industry does Talent XYZ compete in?" asked Sarah.

"We compete in the HRM software development industry. We also sell services such as Integration and Maintenance and Support." said Nils.

"Now let us identify the main factors in the industry that influence Talent XYZ's profitability. Using Porter's five forces framework, we divide them into industry rivals or competitors, customers, suppliers, substitutes, and potential entrants." she continued.

"Our industry rivals are Potential Software, Sophomore, and Xcon (fictitious names). They all manufacture similar products." said Chad.

"Our customers are B2B. They include large and medium corporates." said Divine.

"Our suppliers are Amazon Web Services (AWS) offering its public cloud platform and IT service companies from India such as Ace Consulting Services and Technosys who help us with integration of software into the customer environments." said Rohan.

"Potential entrants are the new digital startups who can offer a similar product with sophisticated features based on the latest digital technologies." said Louise.

"Now let us take each force and analyze them one by one. First, the Threat of New Entrants. We got an aggregate rating of 3.7, which is moderate. Can you explain how?" asked Sarah.

> In our market, we sell customized software to our customers. There are two components in our product. One is the core, which comprises 90 percent of the source code and second is the variable or customizable, which makes up the remaining 10 percent. The cost of development of core component is impacted by the economies of scale. The more customer contracts we win, it will be cheaper to develop the core component. So, for a new entrant, it would be expensive to enter as the upfront capital costs would be high. The major cost will be the tool development from scratch, which is common in the industry. After that, there will be incremental development costs, which are not significant as compared to the initial development costs.
>
> said Victor.

> The switching costs for the customer to move from one product to another would be moderate. Our product is well integrated into the customer environment and interacts with several other applications. Replacing our product means doing the integration and configuration activity all over again for the new product.
>
> said Rahul.

"Are there any incumbency advantages that you have which the new entrants don't?" asked Sarah.

"We have been in this business for two decades. We have built good relationships with our customers. That's the advantage we have over the new players." replied Dirk.

"We are in B2B and do direct sales to our customers and not through distribution channels. The ease of doing business in the EU, Nordics is high." said Anna.

"The exit costs from industry are moderate. One can exit by selling the product to some other company and after doing the necessary knowledge transfer. The industry growth is moderate, neither fast nor slow." replied Mikael.

Sarah continued:

"Next, let's have a look at the Bargaining Power of Suppliers. We got an aggregate rating of 2.1, which is low. Can you explain how?"

We are currently using the AWS cloud platform and migrated a few applications to it. It would be moderately expensive to switch to competitors such as Google Cloud or Microsoft Azure. Our cloud strategy is to go with a hybrid cloud model built into our datacenters. The suppliers have less industry dominance with less control over price as they don't provide a unique product or service. The IT Service industry is competitive and there are many suppliers available in the market, who can support us. Also, there are many substitutes available.

replied Emelie.

"Thanks, Emelie! Can you explain the moderate rating of 4 for the Bargaining Power of Buyers?" asked Sarah.

Our product was the first one in the market to provide an integration of all the HRM processes. But now there are similar products available. Our customers are spread across different industries. They have a good amount of dominance as the vendor switching costs are not very high.

said Nils.

"Next, we move to the substitutes. Are there any substitutes for your software?" asked Sarah. "The only substitute that I can think of is an Excel sheet, too manual and cumbersome to use. We have moved forward from the manual times. There would be hardly anyone using it." said Peter.

"I beg to differ. But you might be surprised to find out that there are still many who use Excel sheets for managing the processes." said Sarah.

She continued "Finally, we come to the industry competitors. You are an incumbent belonging to the IT industry. Your competitors are the front-runners, incumbents as well as entrepreneurs. Let us do a group activity. List down all the front-runners, incumbents, and entrepreneurs in your industry and answer the four key questions for each of them:

1. What value do they provide to their customers in your industry? Do they provide value through a new product, service, experience, or a combination of all three?
2. How do they interact with their customers?
3. How do they generate revenue?
4. What is their cost structure?"

Following were the responses:

	1.	2.	3.	4.
Front-runners: AWS, Microsoft Azure, Google Cloud	They offer public cloud services such as compute, storage, networking, analytics, and security offering low costs of operations. They offer value through low operational costs offering a combination of all three	They have dedicated sales and support teams that interact with their customers	They bill the customers per usage. Different services have different billing structures	They have invested huge capital in building datacenters or regions across the globe
Incumbents: Potential software, Sophomore, Xcon	Their product offers a unification of all the human resources management processes end-to-end. Customers don't need to buy different tools to manage different processes. They provide value not through a completely new product but through incremental versions of their existing one	Through dedicated sales and support teams	They have separate revenue streams for software and services	40% of costs come from product development, 45% from service delivery, 10% from sales, and 5% are miscellaneous admin and overhead costs
Entrepreneurs: iHuman, Tumba	Their product offers features and functionalities developed using the latest digital technologies such as AI and Automation. They provide value through a combination of all three	Through direct sales	They have separate revenue streams for software and services. They sell their software using an annual subscription model	45% of costs come from product development, 20% from service delivery, 30% from sales, and 5% are miscellaneous admin and overhead costs

The workshop participants took a short coffee break and got back to the meeting room. Sarah explained the concept of Customer

Base Audit. Her presentation was well received by the audience as it opened a new perspective of looking at company data. She started a group activity.

"Can you please list the names of all your customers?" asked Sarah.

In total, we have 10 customers. Our biggest customer is Haveth International, one of the largest pharmaceutical companies in Europe. They have been using our product for over a decade. It is an account that fetches us millions of euros per year.

said Chad.

Next ones are Xylem & Phloem, a life sciences company based in Nordics, X-dent, a company offering dental care services in the Nordics, Winner, a sporting goods company based in Finland, Mobicota, a Swedish telecommunications operator, Triumph, one of the largest insurance providers in Nordics, Bilbil, an auto dealer based in Sweden, Acu, one of the largest consumer goods retailers in Sweden, Freya, one of the largest consumer goods retailers in Oslo, and TechHarvest Software, one of the largest IT consulting companies in Scandinavia.

said Nils.

"What is your revenue model?" asked Sarah.

The customers pay for a perpetual software license based on number of users. Also, there is a one-time deployment fee that includes customization, installation, and configuration. Then we charge annual fees for Application Development and Maintenance (ADM), which includes ongoing development and a 24x7 operational support. A major portion of our revenue comes from the recurrent ADM fees.

said Emelie.

Sarah projected the Customer Base Audit sheet on the screen and asked the audience to populate it. Following were the responses from the team.

(in million EUR)

List of customers	Revenues current year	Revenues previous year	Profits current year	Profits previous year	Tickets raised current year	Tickets raised previous year	Tickets resolved current year	Tickets resolved previous year	Number of SLA breaches current year	Number of SLA breaches previous year
Haveth Int	20	20	6.1	6	68	21	19	21	21	0
X&P	20	20	5.8	5	62	23	23	23	19	0
X-dent	19	19	3.95	3.8	71	34	25	34	22	0
Winner	18.5	18.5	2.95	2.9	20	32	19	32	0	1
Mobicota	18	18	2.66	2.65	26	34	25	30	0	1
Triumph	8	8	1.15	1.12	15	32	14	32	1	1
Bilbil	8.5	9	1.12	1.15	23	34	23	31	1	1
Acu	8	8	1.1	1.11	18	23	18	23	1	2
Freya	10	10	1.1	1.1	98	34	35	29	32	1
TechHarvest	10	9.5	1.09	1.05	78	39	33	33	25	1
Total	140	140	27.02	25.88	479	306	234	288	122	8

"Our top five customers are Haveth International, X&P, X-dent, Winner, and Mobicota with a combined revenue of 95.5 M EUR, 68.2 percent of total revenue, both current and previous year." said Dario.

"That's the catch! If you are a company selling services, for a customer base audit, instead of looking at the revenue we look at the customer interactions and the experience, which in our case is the number of tickets raised." said Sarah.

The tickets raised are high compared to the previous year for Haveth International, X&P, X-dent, Freya, and TechHarvest. They also show a high number of Service Level Agreement (SLA) breaches. These are your vulnerable customers. You might lose them sooner if you don't resolve the issues with them. Let's label the remaining: Winner, Mobicota, Triumph, Bilbil, and Acu as our best customers. Why is the number of tickets raised so high for the vulnerable customers?

We had a data breach. Our security systems installed at the customer site became vulnerable to cyber-attacks. We had to change our security software and it costed us millions. That's why you see a steep rise in the number of support tickets and SLA breaches this year.

said Sandeep.

"Now let us only focus on the best customers." said Sarah. "The revenues Talent XYZ earned from them is almost 61 M EUR, both current and last years. Your profit last year was 8.93 M EUR and current year is 8.98 M EUR. Almost all the tickets raised current and last year are resolved. Let us do the following activity in a group with your team.

Discuss the answers to generic questions below for your best customer base:

- What are the new needs or requirements of your customers?
- What does their behavior tell you?
- Are they profitable? How can you improve the profitability?
- How do you connect with your customers?
- How do you interact with them?
- What new digital products and services would you like to offer to them? What experience would it create? What value would it add?"

"Our best customers need personalization and analytics on our software offerings." said Takeaki.

"How do you know?" asked Sarah.

Last month, we had meetings with all of them. They often say that we don't feel a connection with your tool as compared to our other vendors. We feel we have good control over data when we use other tools. It is easier to generate reports and receive recommendations.

said Chad.

We have gained their trust as we have been serving them for more than 5 years. They are our profitable customers, and we have a good relationship with them. I agree with Sarah that we might start losing them soon if we don't digitalize our products and discover a new way of doing business.

said Louise.

"We really need to add AI capabilities to our products." said Prashant.

"We need to find new ways of connecting and interacting with them. But not sure how to begin." said Divine.

"We all need to start with a mindset. I would like to narrate you a story." said Sarah.

She continued:

Sergio Restrepo, the Vice President of Innovation, at Luker Chocolate, a Columbian brand selling chocolate as an ingredient to other food businesses, observed that its sales team was more focused on selling commodity products with volume discounts to the customers. They didn't know much about the customer business. Like a typical B2B company, it measured its KPI on the tons of chocolate sold. It didn't try to understand what the customer needs were and what were their buying behaviors. Luker revised its strategy. It changed its mindset from B2B—Business-to-Business to B4B—Business-for-Business. Instead of thinking itself as a business that sold to other businesses, it started thinking itself as a business that worked for other businesses. Its main KPIs were not the sales of their own products, but how to make the customer grow. Luker had a small cookie company as its customer. Instead of just being a supplier, who supplies them chocolates, it began to act like a consultant to their business. It offered them help in improving the production process and designing a better factory. Luker also started sharing with them new marketing insights and offering help on designing the new packaging. This helped them get into business with a major retail outlet in Canada. Luker also helped them with innovations and connected with some potential customers. In less than nine months, Luker's sales to the cookie company were more than doubled.[1]

"Now let us focus on the vulnerable customers." said Sarah.

The revenues Talent XYZ earned from them is almost 79 M EUR, both current and last years. Your profit current year is 18.04 M EUR and last year was 16.95 M EUR.

Now discuss the answers to the questions below in your group for your vulnerable customer base:

- What are the new needs or requirements of your customers?
- What does their behavior tell you?
- How do you connect with your customers?

- How do you interact with them?
- Are they profitable? If not, do you consider eliminating them?
- If not, how would you restore the relationship with them?

"Due to the data breach issue, we have lost trust with them. It has impacted the relationship adversely. We can be out any time soon." said Mikael.

"But they would think twice before swapping us out as it will not be cheaper to do so." said Dirk.

"Hope they like our new security software." said Rohan.

"I got to know from sources that some of them are even thinking of terminating the ADM contract." said Sandeep.

"That would be a huge revenue loss for us." said Dario.

"ADM is the only lifeline for our company. If that gets severed, there will be blood everywhere. We will soon see trouble." said Nils.

"We need to find our new ways of connecting and interacting with them and restoring our relationships," said Cathrine.

"But how?" asked Peter.

"That's the challenge." said Nils. "In summary, digitalization of our product is a necessity for our survival." said Nils.

To cool off the heated discussion, Sarah called in for a break.

The next topic on her agenda was the Process Analysis.

Following main processes were identified by the leadership teams of Talent XYZ:

- Customer PO
- Invoicing
- Customer cold calling
- Procurement
- Employee travel claims
- Hiring and Selection
- Maintenance and Support Level 1

The Customer PO process at Talent XYZ is as follows:

1. The procurement team of the customer e-mails the PO to the Account Manager at Talent XYZ. Account Manager forwards the PO to the order management desk, a subunit in Talent XYZ's finance team. PO is checked for errors. If there are errors, the order desk notifies the sales team. The sales team then informs the customer. The customer then makes corrections and sends the corrected PO.

2. If there are no errors, then the sales team is notified accordingly by the order desk. The sales team then informs the delivery team about the scope of work, keeping all the heads of different teams in CC.

3. A contract handshake meeting then happens between the sales and delivery team, where the scope of work and detailed terms and conditions of the contract are discussed. The team then begins with the service delivery.

The Invoicing process at Talent XYZ is as follows:

1. Once either a full or partial delivery milestone is complete, a completion or an acceptance certificate is issued by the customer to the sales team at Talent XYZ. It is then forwarded to the finance team.

2. Then, the finance team issues the customer invoice, keeping the sales team in the loop. The invoice specifies the number of credit days as 30. It means that payment is due within the next 30 days.

3. Sales team is notified once the payment is received and then the sales cycle is closed.

4. If the payment is not received within 30 days, then a first payment reminder is sent. If no payment is received within two weeks of the first reminder, then a second reminder is sent. If the payment is still not received within two weeks of the second reminder, then a third and final reminder is sent. If no payment is received within two weeks of the final reminder, then the invoice is handed over to the external debt collection agency.

The Customer cold calling process at Talent XYZ is as follows:

1. The marketing team for each market maintains a list in Excel containing the leads or the names of the prospective customers.
2. More details on the customer's company are acquired by visiting the website and more details on the personal customer contact are acquired through LinkedIn profile.
3. A connect request is sent on LinkedIn along with a personal note. A lead is followed up for two to three weeks. If no active response, then he or she is not contacted further.
4. But if the person is interested, then the interested lead is transferred to the sales.

The Procurement process at Talent XYZ is as follows:

1. The business team that wants to raise a PO contacts the procurement team at Talent XYZ, which is a subunit in finance.
2. The procurement team forwards the request to the Head of Finance for approval.
3. Once the Head of Finance approves, a PO is prepared.
4. It is then e-mailed to the vendor keeping the business team point of contact in CC.

The Employee travel claims process at Talent XYZ is as follows:

1. An employee opens an expense claim form in Excel and fills in all the details. All the expense items need a receipt. An employee must manually scan a copy of the receipts and upload it along with the main claim report.
2. An employee then e-mails the receipts to the travel and expense team in finance.
3. The team goes through all the expense items to check if they are complying with the company's travel policies.

4. If there is a discrepancy, an employee is asked for additional information. If an employee is unable to provide the additional information, then the matter is escalated to the Head of Finance for approval. If the Head of Finance approves, the claim is cleared else, it is rejected.
5. If all the expense items in the report are supported by the scanned receipts, then the claim is labeled as cleared.
6. The payroll team is informed about the reimbursement.
7. The claim is reimbursed in the employee's next salary.

The Hiring and Selection process at Talent XYZ is as follows:

1. The hiring manager from the business team fills up a requisition form with the HR, explaining the name of the new job and the business purpose.
2. It goes to the business unit head and HR head for approval.
3. If either of them disapproves, then no requisition is created. If both approve, then a job ID is created. HR team contacts the hiring manager and asks for more job description details such as title, responsibilities, core competencies, educational background, skills, personal characteristics, and compensation.
4. The HR then posts the job on the company's job portal and other job portals such as LinkedIn for a specific number of days.
5. The HR is notified via e-mail once a resume is received from an interested candidate.
6. The resumes are then shortlisted manually, and the selected candidates are contacted for an HR interview.
7. Once the candidate clears the HR interview, his/her profile is sent to the hiring manager for the next round of interview.
8. Once the candidate clears the interview, the candidate is given an offer.
9. The candidate must accept or decline within a week. If the candidate accepts the offer, then the start date is agreed upon and the onboarding is scheduled.

The Maintenance and Support Level 1 process at Talent XYZ is as follows:

1. Customer calls the Talent XYZ customer care.
2. Call is answered by the Level 1 support team and the troubleshooting begins. The level 1 team makes the best effort to resolve the issues on the phone.
3. If they are unable to resolve, then it is escalated to the level 2 support team.

"Let us start rating these processes." said Sarah.

The Customer PO process has a customer touchpoint. It is inter functional as it involves sales, delivery, and finance. It is moderately expensive as it has five full-time employees from the order desk dedicated to it. It is not very complex. It could be time-consuming depending on the workload. The bottleneck lies with the order management desk. The turn-around time between forwarding the PO to the order management desk and returning it back to the sales team can be anywhere between 1 hour to 2 days depending on the workload. It needs lots of manual intervention. It is repetitive and administrative.

said Dirk.

The Invoicing process has a customer touchpoint. It is inter functional as it needs the involvement of finance and sales. It is moderately expensive as it has two full-time employees from finance dedicated to it. It is not a complex process. It could be time-consuming depending on the workload. The bottlenecks lie between receiving an acceptance certificate from the customer, which can take up to 1 to 5 business days and forwarding the acceptance certificate to the finance and creating an invoice for the customers, which can take up to 1 hour to 2 working days. It needs manual intervention. It is repetitive and administrative.

said Dario.

The Customer cold calling process has a customer touchpoint. It is intra functional as it is mainly driven by sales. It is moderately expensive as the customer acquisition costs can be sometimes high. It is not so complex. But it can be time-consuming. The sales cycle can be as long as 3 to 6 months. It needs manual intervention. It is repetitive. It is partially administrative.

said Mikael.

The Procurement process does not have a customer touchpoint. It is inter functional involving finance and business. It is moderately expensive as it has three full-time employees from finance dedicated to it. It is not a complex process. It is not time-consuming either. It is repetitive, administrative, and needs manual intervention.

said Dario.

The Employee travel and expense process is internal with no customer touchpoint. It is inter functional which involves finance and employees from all over the organization. It is moderately expensive as it has three full-time employees from finance dedicated to it. It is not so complex. The bottleneck lies with finance from 1 to 2 business days depending on the workload. It is repetitive, administrative, and manual.

said Dario.

The Hiring and Selection process does not have a customer touchpoint. It is inter functional involving HR and hiring managers from different teams. It is costly as it has fifteen people from HR dedicated full-time to it. It also includes high employee acquisition costs. It is moderately complex and time-consuming as shortlisting and interviewing the candidates can be complicated and take a lot of time. It is manual, repetitive, and administrative.

said Cathrine.

The Maintenance and Support Level 1 process has a customer touchpoint. It is intra functional. It is costly as it has a team of 45 full-time dedicated employees. It is a straightforward process and not very complex. The bottleneck lies in issue resolution which depends on the SLA. Severity 1 issues to be resolved within 2 hours. Severity 2 issues to be resolved between 4 hours to 48 hours. Severity 3 issues to the resolved within 24 hours to 5 business days. It is manual and repetitive. It is nonadministrative as it is driven by the business.

said Sandeep.

Following was the average of the scoring sheets filled in by the workshop attendees.

Process	Customer touchpoints	Inter functional	Costs	Complexity	Time-consuming	Manual intervention	Repetitive	Administrative	Score
Customer PO	5	5	3	1	3	5	5	5	32
Invoicing	5	4	2	1	3	5	5	5	30
Customer cold calling	4	2	3	1	4	4	4	1	23
Procurement	1	4	3	1	2	5	5	5	26
Employee travel claims	1	3	3	1	2	5	5	5	25
Hiring and Selection	1	3	5	3	4	5	5	5	31
Maintenance and Support Level 1	5	2	5	2	3	5	5	1	28

"From the scoring sheet, we infer that the main three processes to be automated are Customer PO, Hiring and Selection, and Invoicing." said Sarah.

Next, she began with the People Analysis.

"How many employees work at Talent XYZ?" asked Sarah. "We are a workforce of 2500 employees." replied Cathrine.

Sarah said:

Let us fill in the knowledge matrix. Make a list of all the main business jobs at your firm. Then, map each job to the following knowledge areas: Product/Service knowledge, Portfolio-wide knowledge, Digital technologies knowledge, Industry knowledge, and Customer-specific knowledge. If a particular knowledge area applies to a specific job, then put 'X'. Otherwise, leave it blank.

The knowledge matrix was as follows:

	Product/ Service knowledge	Portfolio-wide knowledge	Digital technologies knowledge	Industry knowledge	Customer-specific knowledge
Software Developer	X	X	X		
Technical SME	X	X	X	X	X
Software Sales Support Manager		X		X	X
Test Engineer	X		X		
System Analyst	X	X	X		
Manager-Design		X		X	X
Manager-Testing		X		X	X
Director-Product Development		X		X	X
Director-Presales Support Software		X		X	X
Head of Business Unit Software				X	X
Installation Engineer	X	X	X		
Configuration Engineer	X	X	X		
Consultant	X	X	X	X	X
Service Sales Support Manager		X		X	X
Level 1 Support Specialist	X	X			
Level 2 Support Specialist	X	X	X		
Manager-Install		X	X	X	
Manager-Configure		X	X	X	
Manager Level 1 Support		X		X	
Manager Level 2 Support		X		X	
Director-Integration				X	X

	Product/ Service knowledge	Portfolio- wide knowledge	Digital technologies knowledge	Industry knowledge	Customer- specific knowledge
Director-Maintenance and Support				X	X
Director-Presales Support Services				X	X
Head of Business Unit Services				X	X
Account Manager		X		X	X
Sales Director		X		X	X
Key Account Manager (KAM)		X		X	X
Head of Sales				X	X

Business Unit Software Jobs

- Head of Business Unit Software: Responsible for profit and loss of the entire unit.

Product Development

- Software Developer: To code and develop software features and functionalities.
- Test Engineer: To test software features and functionalities.
- Manager-Design: To lead the team of software developers.
- Manager-Testing: To lead the team of software test engineers.
- Director-Product Development: To lead the product development unit.

Presales Support Software

- System Analyst: To translate customer specific business requirements into functional requirements.
- Software Sales Support Manager: Offer commercial support for software sales.
- Technical SME: Offer technical support during presales.
- Director-Presales Support Software: To lead the presales software support unit.

Business Unit Services Jobs

- Head of Business Unit Services: Responsible for profit and loss of the entire unit.

Integration

- Installation Engineer: To install software in a customer environment.
- Configuration Engineer: To configure and make the software go live in a customer environment.
- Manager-Install: To lead the team of installation engineers.
- Manager-Configure: To lead the team of configuration engineers.
- Director-Integration: To lead the integration unit.

Maintenance and Support

- Level 1 Support Specialist: To offer 1st line of support to customers.
- Level 2 Support Specialist: To offer 2nd line of support to customers.
- Manager Level 1 Support: To lead the team of level 1 support specialists.
- Manager Level 2 Support: To lead the team of level 2 support specialists.
- Director-Maintenance and Support: To lead the maintenance and support team.

Presales Support Services

- Consultant: To offer consulting to customers during product and service sales.
- Service Sales Support Manager: To offer commercial support during service sales.
- Director-Presales Support Services: To lead the presales support services team.

Sales Jobs

- Account Manager/Sales Director—Responsible for selling and managing relationships with new and existing customers.
- KAM—Profit and Loss (P&L) responsible for a specific customer account and lead a team of Account Managers and Sales Directors.
- Head of Sales—Responsible for P&L of all the customer accounts.

"Now fill in the current and future, technical and nontechnical skills, in your organization in the matrix below and answer the five generic questions." said Sarah.

1. What is the new digital competence required?
2. How to transition from current to new competence?
3. What new jobs will be created in the future?
4. What current jobs will be eliminated?
5. To establish a learning culture, how do we make sure we:
   a. Encourage and motivate people to learn.
   b. Develop a clear learning plan or pathway for everyone.
   c. Access the latest digital learning tools.
   d. Establish a continuous learning check-in process.
   e. Set up a learning and development governance at all levels in our organization.

Following was the skills matrix filled in by Talent XYZ.

	Technical skills	**Nontechnical skills**
Current	• Software Development • Software Testing • System Engineering • Database Management • Storage Management • Network Engineering • IT Administration • Datacenter Management • Process Modeling	• Project Management • Program Management • Strategy • Consulting • Sales • Accounting • Marketing

(Continues)

(*Continued*)

	Technical skills	Nontechnical skills
Future	• Artificial Intelligence • Machine Learning • Automation • Data Science	• Digital Leadership • Digital Strategy • Digital Marketing

"We need new digital competence in the areas of AI and Automation." said Prashant.

"We should plan some upskilling and reskilling programs to transition from current to new competence." said Cathrine.

"The new future jobs will be AI Developer, Automation Specialist, and Data Scientist." said Rohan.

"We need to have another look at the customer requirements and our internal organization structures to understand which jobs we can merge or eliminate. We should think about investing in digital learning and development to create a continuous learning culture." said Nils.

Next Sarah started with Data Analysis. Following was the combined response:

1. Data flow at customer touchpoints

Customer Touchpoints	Data flowing IN	Data flowing OUT
Lead	High level description of lead, point of contact at customer	Company info, product/service description, point of contact at Talent XYZ
Opportunity	Customer requirements, deal size, business value to customer, timelines	Business case, scope of work, technical solution, delivery timelines, team competence
Contract	Signed copy of contract	Signed copy of contract
Order	PO	Quotation
Delivery	Customer feedback, signoffs, phase approvals	Agreed deliverables
Acceptance	Acceptance certificate	Acceptance certificate request
Invoice	Invoice acknowledgment	Invoice
Payment	Payment transfer notification	Payment reminders

2. Data flow in between the functions/units

Data flow in between functions/units	Business unit software	Business unit services	Finance	Marketing	HR	IT
Sales	Contract details, product releases, training, new sales opportunities	Contract details, project reviews, new sales opportunities	PO, invoices, project reviews, budget	Leads	Hiring, onboarding, rewards, appraisals, training, exiting	IT updates
Business unit software		Product releases, training	Budget	X	Hiring, onboarding, rewards, appraisals, training, exiting	IT updates
Business unit services	X		Budget	X	Hiring, onboarding, rewards, appraisals, training, exiting	IT updates
Finance	X	X		Budget	Hiring, onboarding, rewards, appraisals, training, exiting	IT updates, budget
Marketing	X	X	X		Hiring, onboarding, rewards, appraisals, training, exiting	IT updates
HR	X	X	X	X		IT updates, hiring, onboarding, rewards, appraisals, training, exiting

3. Data flow within functions/units

Functions	Data flow
Sales	Leads, new opportunities, orders booked, net sales booked, work in progress, customer information, contracts, P&L, sales reviews, OPEX
Business Unit Software	Product releases, product development plans, technical documentation, sales reviews, P&L, OPEX
Business Unit Services	Project delivery, issues and escalations, SLA reviews, sales reviews, P&L, OPEX
Finance	Payroll, accounts, taxation, compliance, annual reports, P&L reviews, budget reviews, procurements
Marketing	Leads, product campaigns, market research and development, budget
HR	Hiring, onboarding, training, employee motivation plan, appraisals, compensations, employee retention plan, exiting
IT	IT tools development and maintenance procedures, updates, upgrades, performance metrics, budget

Then she asked everyone to answer the following questions for all the data flow types in sheets 1, 2, and 3.

a. Is this data sensitive? What portions of data are to be kept private and confidential?
b. Is the data fluid? What are the systems, units, tools, etc. impacted by this data currently, and what could be impacted in the future?
c. Is it easy to gather data from multiple sources? If not, what are the challenges? How can these challenges be overcome?
d. What real-time metrics can be generated from this data? Who would be the target audience?
e. Can this data generate valuable insights? What value can it add to the business?

Following were the responses to the above questions presented in a tabular format:

Sheet 1: Data flow at customer touchpoints

Customer touchpoints	a.	b.	c.	d.	e.
Lead	No	Yes, to be shared between marketing and sales	Easy to gather	• Number of leads generated	Yes, all the data can generate valuable insights
Opportunity	Yes, whole data	Yes, to be shared between sales, BU: software, and BU: services	Easy to gather	• Number of leads converted to opportunities • % of leads converted to opportunities	
Contract	Yes, whole data	Yes, to be shared between sales, BU: software, BU: services, and finance	Easy to gather	• Number of contracts/deals closed	
Order	Yes, whole data	Yes, to be shared between sales, BU: software, BU: services, and finance	Easy to gather	• Number of orders booked	
Delivery	Yes, whole data	Yes, to be shared between sales, BU: software, BU: services, and finance	Easy to gather	• % of projects delivered	
Acceptance	Yes, whole data	Yes, to be shared between sales, BU: software, BU: services, and finance	Easy to gather	• Net Sales recognized • % of orders booked converted to net sales	
Invoice	Yes, whole data	Yes, to be shared between sales and finance	Easy to gather	• Total value of accounts receivable • % of Net Sales invoiced	
Payment	Yes, whole data	No, to be restricted within finance	Easy to gather	• Total cash collected • % of accounts receivables converted to cash	

Sheet 2: Data flow in between functions/units

Data flow in between functions/ units	Business Unit Software	Business Unit Services	Finance	Marketing	HR	IT
Sales	• Only contract details are sensitive data. Rest is nonsensitive • Real-time metrics are: number of contracts signed, value of contracts, number of new releases, number of new sales opportunities	• Contract details and project reviews are sensitive data. Rest is nonsensitive • Real-time metrics are: number of contracts signed, value of contracts, number of new releases, number of new sales opportunities	• Whole data is sensitive • Real-time metrics are: number of orders booked, amount of orders booked, amount of accounts receivable, number of projects on track, % of budget consumed	• Nonsensitive data • Real-time metrics are: number of leads generated, % of leads converted into opportunities	• Hiring, rewards, appraisal, exiting are sensitive • Real-time metrics are: number of hires, onboarding experience, total spend in rewards, number of top performers, amount of budget spent	• Nonsensitive data • Real-time metrics are: Your IT usage meter-memory, CPU, storage

(Continues)

(*Continued*)

Data flow in between functions/ units	Business Unit Software	Business Unit Services	Finance	Marketing	HR	IT
Business Unit Software		• Nonsensitive data • Real-time metrics are: number of product releases, number of training	• Sensitive data • Real-time metrics are amount of budget spent	X		
Business Unit Services	X		• Sensitive data • Real-time metrics are amount of budget spent	X		
Finance	X	X		• Sensitive data • Real-time metrics are amount of budget spent		• Sensitive data • Real-time metrics are: Your IT usage meter-memory, CPU, storage, amount of budget spent
Marketing	X	X	X			• Nonsensitive data • Real-time metrics are: Your IT usage meter-memory, CPU, storage
HR	X	X	X	X		• Only IT updates are nonsensitive data. Hiring, rewards, appraisal, exiting are sensitive • Real-time metrics are: Your IT usage meter-memory, CPU, storage

3. Data flow within functions/units
   Sensitive indicated by "s"

Functions	Data flow
Sales	Leads, new opportunities, orders booked(s), net sales booked(s), work in progress(s), customer information(s), contracts(s), P&L(s), sales reviews(s), OPEX(s)

Functions	Data flow
Business Unit Software	Product releases, product development plans, technical documentation, sales reviews(s), P&L(s), OPEX(s)
Business Unit Services	Project delivery, issues and escalations, SLA reviews(s), sales reviews(s), P&L(s), OPEX(s)
Finance	Payroll, accounts, taxation, compliance, annual reports, P&L reviews, budget reviews, procurements (all sensitive)
Marketing	Leads, product campaigns, market research and development, budget(s)
HR	Hiring(s), onboarding, training, employee motivation plan, appraisals(s), compensations(s), employee retention plan, exiting(s)
IT	It tools development and maintenance procedures, updates, upgrades, performance metrics, budget(s)

Sarah then began with the IT Tools Analysis.

Following was the valuation provided by Talent XYZ for IT tools.

IT tools	Criti- cality	Usage	Evolu- tion	Oper- ational Costs	Secu- rity	Custom- ization	Reus- ability	Inter- face	Redun- dancy	Score
Customer Relationship Management (CRM)	5	5	4	4	4	4	3	5	5	39
Leads Generator	2	2	2	2	3	3	1	2	5	22
Delivery Manager	5	5	4	3	4	4	2	5	5	37
Human Resource Management	4	4	4	3	3	3	1	3	5	30
Accounting and Payroll	5	5	3	3	4	3	1	3	5	32
Invoicing	4	4	3	3	4	3	1	3	5	30
Product Develop- ment Tool	4	4	3	4	3	3	1	3	5	30

Following were the answers to the generic questions:

1. What are the tools with lower and higher scores?

Ans: CRM and Delivery Manager are the tools with the higher score. Leads Generator is the tool with the lower score.

2. What is the cost of maintaining them?

Ans: Costs of operating and maintaining CRM and Delivery Manager are high, whereas Leads Generator is low.

3. Are they developed in-house or purchased from 3rd party?

Ans: All of them are 3rd party.

4. What can we do with them: phase out, replace, or migrate to cloud?

Ans: We can phase out Leads Generator and migrate CRM and Delivery Manager to cloud.

The analysis phase was complete. Sarah prepared the attendees for the next phase- Definition: Developing a Wanted Position.

Following was the response:

Time Frame: 24 months	Current Digital Maturity Level: 1	Future Digital Maturity Level: 3
New Business Adoption	Low	Medium
Digital Technology Adoption	Low	Medium

Then she asked to refer to the results of all the analysis. Following was the response to the questions:

Questions	Responses
How can the current profitability of your industry be improved?	Offer differentiated products and services
How can the weaker forces from Porter's five forces framework be improved?	Industry competition is high, which negatively impacts profitability. It can be improved by offering new differentiated products and services
How can the stronger forces from Porter's five forces framework be leveraged?	Bargaining power of suppliers is low, which positively impacts profitability. It can be leveraged by reducing costs by moving more applications to the cloud. Availability of substitutes is low, which positively impacts profitability. It can be leveraged by offering new differentiated products and services

Questions	Responses
What are the current and future needs of your customers?	Current needs: Personalization and Analytics in products. Future needs: Advanced AI/Machine Learning capabilities
What new personalized experiences can you provide them?	Personalized login portals for users, personalized recommendations
What new digital products and services can you offer them?	Products with AI and Analytics capabilities
Which processes can be automated?	Customer PO, Hiring and Selection, Invoicing
How can the lead times and costs be reduced?	By identifying the bottlenecks, and automating manual and repetitive processes
What is the overall business impact?	Reduced costs, faster lead times, better customer experience
How can we bridge the gap between current and future competence?	Offering upskilling and reskilling programs
What new learning programs do we need to implement?	Competence development programs on Cloud, AI, and Automation
How can we create a learning culture?	Appointing change drivers and champions, strong support from the top management, changing the mindset, learning and development ownership by individuals
How can the data flowing at customer touchpoints add value?	It can help us generate real-time metrics and insights, which can improve customer experience and relationships
How can the data flowing in between the functions add value?	It can break the silos between the teams and help everyone stay on the same page
How can the data flowing within the functions add value?	It can help in better knowledge sharing and asset reuse
How can we derive more value from the tools with higher scores?	Reduce the costs further by migrating them to the cloud

Following was the list of Preliminary Strategic Priorities corresponding to each analysis and a Final Strategic Priority.

Analysis	Preliminary Strategic Priorities	Final Strategic Priorities
Industry/Customer	1. Digitalize products and services 2. Customer engagement through metaverse and chatbots 3. Pilot digital technology use cases for customers	Digitalize products and services
Process	4. Automate wherever possible 5. Automate customer support 6. Invest in automation tools	Automate wherever possible
People	7. Build digital competence 8. Better employee experience through Gamification 9. Invest in Learning and Development	Build digital competence
Data	10. Data-driven decision making 11. Data protection, Data integrity 12. Improve Cybersecurity	Data-driven decision making
IT Tools	13. Invest in AI 14. Procure more IT tools 15. Digitalize core IT	Digitalize core IT

Wanted Position

To be at Level 3 from Level 1 of Digital Maturity in 24 months.

Strategic Priorities

1. Digitalize products and services
2. Automate wherever possible
3. Build digital competence
4. Data-driven decision making
5. Digitalize core IT

"That was the end of Day 1 of the workshop. We meet tomorrow morning for Day 2." said Sarah.

——————x——————

"Good morning! Welcome to Day 2 of the workshop. We shall begin with Strategy Execution. Please use the flowchart below to select a Transformation Type." said Sarah.

"We are not venturing into a new industry. We would like to offer new products and services. We don't want to continue with the current core business. So, it's a Core business transformation." said Nils.

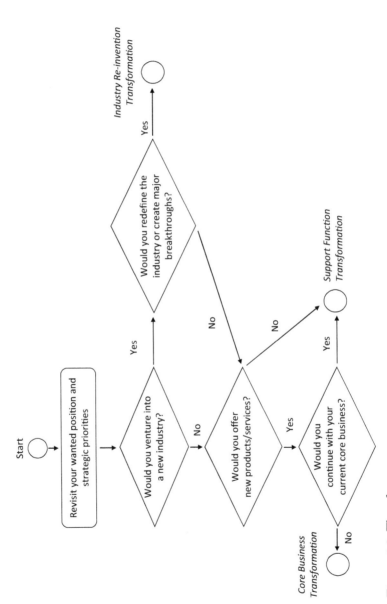

Figure 6.2 Flowchart

Next Sarah started the Business Model selection activity with the group. "There are 5 widely adopted business models: Platform based, Ad-supported, Freemium, Subscription based, Access over ownership. Are you currently using any of these?"

"No." replied Victor.

"Then, I would like to provide you with a set of questions. You have 15 minutes to discuss them in your group." said Sarah.

Following were the responses:

Questions	Responses
Can we change our current business model to Platform based?	No
Do we want to own assets or resources? Can we change our current business model Access over ownership?	No
Do we want to offer free products and services to our customers perpetually? If yes, then can we change our business model to Ad-supported?	No
Do we want to offer free products and services to our customers initially and charge later for premium upgrades? If yes, then can we change our business model to Freemium?	No
Can we change our business model to Subscription based?	Yes. We would like to go for a subscription based, as-a-service business model for our software product. We would no longer offer our software on one-time basis but rather as-a-service Pros: We can generate recurrent revenues. It can improve our revenue forecasts. Customers will always be on the latest software/tool release or version Cons: It will be challenging to renegotiate the contracts with the customers. If they insist on the old model, we cannot fully introduce it. But for our services business, there will be no change. We will continue selling the maintenance and support and integration services as before
Can we combine two or more of the above five business models?	No

Questions	Responses
Can we continue with our current business model?	No, for products. Yes, for services
Is there a new business model, besides the above 5, that we can adopt?	No

Sarah started the next exercise—Selecting the Ecosystem.

"Do you have in mind any ecosystems that you would like to be part of or start your own?" asked Sarah.

"We have heard about the promise of the ecosystems but never explored anything like that before in our business. Can you suggest some ecosystems that would be suitable for us?" asked Divine.

The ecosystem that you can pioneer could be the one with your existing customers who use your product. Let them connect and share the best practices and experiences with one another. Talent XYZ could be the main orchestrator of the ecosystem, managing the information and interactions.

replied Sarah.

"But we have different pricing for our different customers. We have sold them customized products as per their requirements. What if the customers learn this vital piece of information from one another?" asked Chad.

"That's a good question. We don't share sensitive and confidential data and information on the ecosystem. But we can share the product experiences, implementation, and operational best practices, which can be valuable for one another." replied Sarah.

I can recommend some ecosystems where you can be a good follower and seek and share value. We at Digiculum orchestrate ecosystems with software and IT consulting companies in Nordics, mid-size companies from different industries in Europe, and Human resource management team from different companies. It would be beneficial for you to join them where you can understand the challenges and pain points of other players in the ecosystem and modify your products and services accordingly.

"Seems to be a good idea! So, we have 4 ecosystems to evaluate. Let's begin the exercise." said Nils. After 1 hour of evaluation, following was the exercise outcome:

Ecosystems	Objective	Differentiation	Trust	Governance	Flexibility	Score
Talent XYZ Product	4	2	5	4	3	18
Nordics software and IT	3	2	2	3	3	13
Mid-size companies across industries in EU	3	3	3	4	2	15
HR ecosystem	5	4	3	3	3	18

Based on the outcome, it was decided that Talent XYZ would pioneer the Talent XYZ product ecosystem with the support from Digiculum and follow the HR ecosystem.

"Let us identify the Change Areas for the Strategy Execution." said Sarah. "We have the following five strategic priorities: Digitalize products and services, Automate wherever possible, Build digital competence, Digitalize core IT, Data-driven decision making."

"In order to digitalize products and services, we need to redefine our product development methodology. We need to introduce AI capabilities into products." said Takeaki.

"For the strategic priority, Automate wherever possible, let us do a pilot use case with the Customer PO process. We will try to automate the process and note down the efficiency and cost savings." said Anna.

"To build digital competence, we need to introduce new digital competence development programs." said Cathrine.

"For the strategic priority, Data-driven decision making, we need to set up a Data Analytics function to collect data." said Rahul.

"For the strategic priority, Digitalize core IT, let us do a cloud migration program. We can do an assessment of which applications to migrate to Cloud." said Peter.

Thus, the Change Areas for each Strategic Priority were mapped.

Strategic Priorities	Change Areas
Digitalize products and services	Build AI capabilities into products
Build digital competence	Digital competence development programs
Data-driven decision making	Data Analytics function setup
Automate wherever possible	Customer PO process
Digitalize core IT	Migration to Cloud

"So, let us map technologies with the Change Areas." said Sarah.
The Talent XYZ team gave the following in the table form.

Strategic Priorities	Change Areas	Technology Mapping
Digitalize products and services	Build AI capabilities into products	AI
Build digital competence	Digital competence development programs	AI, Cloud, Data Analytics
Data-driven decision making	Data Analytics function setup	Data Analytics
Automate wherever possible	Customer PO process	Automation
Digitalize core IT	Migration to Cloud	Cloud

"Now let us create a business case for each of the Change Areas. You need to calculate the business value and the cost to implement the technology." said Sarah.

The Talent XYZ team gave the following in the table form.

Strategic Priorities	Change Areas	Technology Mapping	Business Value	Cost of Change
Digitalize products and services	Build AI capabilities into products	AI	Increased Revenue (high), Increased Customer Satisfaction (high)	Moderate
Build digital competence	Digital competence development programs	AI, Cloud, Data Analytics	Increased Revenue (moderate), Increased Customer Satisfaction (high)	Moderate

(Continues)

(*Continued*)

Strategic Priorities	Change Areas	Technology Mapping	Business Value	Cost of Change
Data-driven decision making	Data Analytics function setup	Data Analytics	Cost Reduction (high), Increased customer satisfaction (high), Increased revenue (moderate)	Moderate
Automate wherever possible	Customer PO process	Automation	Cost Reduction (moderate)	Moderate
Digitalize core IT	Migration to cloud	Cloud	Cost Reduction (low)	Moderate

The Strategic Priorities: Digitalize products and services, Build digital competence, and Data-driven decision making showed higher business value and moderate costs. Hence a business decision to execute them first was made.

"Let us create Metrics for each of the Strategic Priorities." said Sarah.

Following KPIs were added to the table by Talent XYZ:

Strategic Priorities	Change Areas	Technology Mapping	Business Value	Cost of Change	KPIs
Digitalize products and services	Build AI capabilities into products	AI	Increased Revenue (high), Increased Customer Satisfaction (high)	Moderate	• Number of AI capabilities introduced in products • % Increased revenue
Build digital competence	Digital competence development programs	AI, Cloud, Data Analytics	Increased Revenue (moderate), Increased Customer Satisfaction (high)	Moderate	• Number of employees who completed training per month • Employee feedback score
Data-driven decision making	Data Analytics function setup	Data Analytics	Cost Reduction (high), Increased Customer Satisfaction (high), Increased Revenue (moderate)	Moderate	• Number of business decisions based on Data Analytics
Automate wherever possible	Customer PO process	Automation	Cost Reduction (moderate)	Moderate	• % Reduction in costs
Digitalize core IT	Migration to Cloud	Cloud	Cost Reduction (low)	Moderate	• Number of applications migrated to cloud

Following table shows details on KPIs:

Strategic Priorities	KPI statement	Target	Performance Indicators
Digitalize products and services	Number of AI capabilities introduced in products	20	Off-track—below 20 On-track—between 20 and 30 Stretch—above 30
	% Increased revenue	Above 10%	Off-track—below 10% On-track—between 10% and 15% Stretch—above 15%
Build digital competence	Number of employees who completed training per month	Between 25 and 50	Off-track—below 25 On-track—between 25 and 50 Stretch—above 50
	Employee feedback score	Score 6 on a scale of 1 to 10 (10-highest, 1-lowest)	Off-track—Score 5 and below On-track—Score between 6 and 8 Stretch—Scores 9 and 10
Data-driven decision making	Number of business decisions based on Data Analytics	Between 5 and 10	Off-track—below 5 On-track—between 5 to 10 Stretch—above 10
Automate wherever possible	% Reduction in costs	Between 25% and 35%	Off-track—below 25% On-track—between 25% and 35% Stretch—above 35%
Digitalize core IT	Number of applications migrated to cloud	Between 10 and 20	Off-track—below 10 On-track—between 10 and 20 Stretch—above 20

This was the end of the two-day workshop with the Talent XYZ leaders. Sarah guided them through the Strategy Creation and the Planning phase of Strategy Execution. The next big challenge before them was the Delivery phase. Sarah and her team offered 90-day support on Dashboard Monitoring and Continuous Improvement.

"Thank you so much Sarah for the workshop." said Nils on behalf of the entire team.

"It is just the beginning. I wish you good luck with the Digital Transformation. We are here to support you." said Sarah.

We are your transformation partners.

APPENDIX

Digital Technologies

We shall discuss the following digital technologies shown in Figure A.1.

AI	Automation	Data Science and Data Analytics	Blockchain	IoT
5G	Cloud	Gamification	Extended Reality	Metaverse

Figure A.1 Digital Technologies

Artificial Intelligence (AI)

The concept of AI has been existing for 70 years but with the rising wave of Digital Transformation, the business application of AI has become very significant. AI is a group of technologies that enable machines to work with a higher level of intelligence and simulate human capabilities to sense, comprehend, and act.

The global enterprise adoption of AI is projected to grow at a compound annual growth rate of 38.1 percent.[1] As per research conducted by MIT Sloan on top reasons why the firms are interested in AI:

- 84 percent of firms believe that AI will allow them to obtain or sustain a competitive advantage.
- 75 percent say that AI will allow them to move into new businesses.
- 75 percent of firms believe that AI will safeguard them against the threat of new players entering the market segment.
- 63 percent say that the pressure to reduce costs will allow them to use AI.
- 61 percent believe that AI will enable supplier compatibility.
- 59 percent believe that AI will enable customer willingness.[2]

In a global survey of 3,100 business executives conducted by MIT and Boston Consulting Group,[3] based on the understanding and adoption of AI, the firms can be classified as:

- Passives
- Experimenters
- Investigators
- Pioneers

Passives have a low understanding and low adoption of AI.

Experimenters have a low understanding but high adoption of AI.

Investigators have a high understanding but low adoption of AI.

Pioneers have a high understanding and high adoption of AI.

Among the Nordic companies surveyed, the distribution was relatively even with Passives 22 percent, Experimenters 30 percent, Investigators 22 percent, and Pioneers 26 percent.[4]

Some of the top challenges faced by the firms in adopting AI are:

1. Attracting, acquiring, and developing the right talent
2. Competing investment policies within a firm
3. Security concerns
4. Cultural resistance
5. Limited technology capabilities
6. Lack of leadership support for AI initiatives
7. Unclear or no business case for AI applications[5]

AI has a strong impact on business areas: Customer Engagement and Internal Operations.

And within Internal Operations, AI can impact all the functional areas. However, its impact on Sales and Marketing, IT, Supply, and HR is relatively higher.

It is predicted that as AI platforms become more powerful sales and marketing mediums, customers will shift their focus from trusted brands to trusted AI platform. It means as a customer you do not have to worry about selecting which brands are best suited to your needs. You just need to select a trusted platform that knows you very well and selects the brand

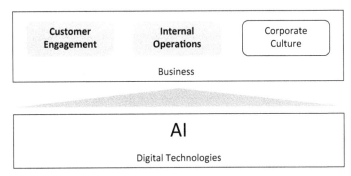

Figure A.2 Business impact of AI

for you. This will strongly impact customer acquisition. Issues with customer acquisition today are that lots of money is spent on ads that don't often reach the right customers. They are contacted via multiple advertising channels such as TV, Internet, radio, print, and so on. AI platforms will analyze the customer needs, touch points, references, buying behaviors, and pricing characteristics and make sure that the right brands are directed to them at the right time and just through a single channel, which is AI platform.[6]

IT services portfolio includes infrastructure, platforms, and software applications and there are various business models such as Infrastructure-as-a-Service or IaaS, Platform-as-a-service or PaaS, and Software-as-a-service or SaaS. AI can make an impact at various layers in the service portfolio.

AI can impact Supply in Demand Forecasting, Procurement, and Logistics. In *Demand Forecasting*, AI can forecast how many products are needed from various suppliers in advance based on data points such as previous spread, inventory, supplier product catalog, and customer needs. In *Procurement*, AI can help to select the best offer from various vendors based on various comparison parameters such as prices, vendor credibility, performance, market demands, and so on. In *Logistics*, AI can work out the most efficient shipping and delivery options for the supply of goods.[7]

AI has strong use cases in HR. AI can help managers reduce bias in the hiring and selection process by shortlisting candidates based on background factors such as education and experience and personal factors such as intellectual ability, personality, and motivation. It can ensure that good candidates are not screened out too early in this selection process. AI can also provide recommendations to managers about what kind of competencies they should look for in a candidate for a specific job, based on performance and attribute data of previous candidates.[8]

Figure A.3 shows the AI capabilities and building blocks.[9]

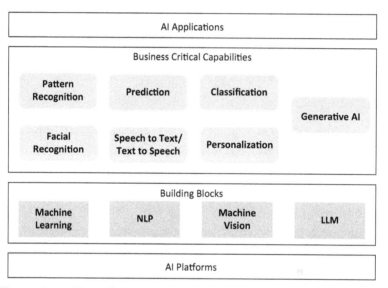

Figure A.3 AI capabilities and building blocks

AI platform consists of four main building blocks:

1. Machine Learning
2. Natural Language Processing (NLP)
3. Machine Vision
4. Large Language Models (LLM)

Machine Learning is the ability to learn from data without being explicitly programed.

NLP is the ability to understand and interpret the intent behind the human language.

Machine Vision is the ability to detect and recognize faces and objects in an image.

LLM are deep learning algorithms that have the ability to recognize, summarize, translate, predict, and generate human-like content using very large datasets.

These building blocks can be used independently or together to build an AI capability.

A *Capability* is defined as the operational tasks to be performed by the machine that adds value to the business. There are seven business-critical capabilities:

1. Pattern Recognition
2. Prediction
3. Classification
4. Facial Recognition
5. Speech to Text/Text to Speech
6. Personalization
7. Generative AI

Pattern Recognition is the ability to identify a consistent or repeatable pattern based on various data points.

Prediction is the ability to offer a forecast based on observed patterns or collected data points.

Classification is the ability to segregate the data or information objects based on certain characteristics.

Facial recognition is the ability to identify a person based on facial expressions and understand his emotional state based on the different facial expressions.

Speech to Text/ Text to Speech is the ability to transform spoken words into text/written text into speech.

Personalization is the ability to offer personal recommendations to the user based on his/her preferences.

Generative AI is the ability to generate a new text, image, or other form of content using generative models.

An AI application is built by combining one or more business capabilities based on the business problem to be solved.

Automation

Automation is a digital technology that automates business processes based on the notion of software robots or simply bots. A bot is a software code that is inserted into the IT application environment without affecting its underlying infrastructure.

There are two kinds of Automation:

- Rule-based Automation
- AI-driven Automation

Rule-based Automation is a framework that tells a system how to respond to certain events, if or when they occur. The interaction is simple- when X happens perform Y action. The programer must explicitly program the rules. It is mainly used for tasks that are administrative, repetitive, and need long manual working hours. Rule-based Automation is further classified into Robotic Process Automation (RPA) and Run Book Automation (RBA). *RPA* uses preprogramed software that allows to automate activities, transactions, and tasks in one or more IT systems. RPA requires structured data and predefined utilization rules and allows us to automate mundane tasks. *RBA* is defined as a set of procedures defined in run books that are developed by the administrator or IT professional for maintaining the everyday routine as well as the exceptional operation of a computer system or network. For example, it includes procedures such as starting or stopping the system instructions for handling special devices, procedures for how to perform backups, and so on.

In *AI-driven* Automation, bots are intelligent algorithms that learn from various datasets and data patterns and can take an appropriate decision or action when the underlying environments or conditions change.[10]

As shown in Figure A.4, Automation has an impact on Customer Engagement and Internal Operations.

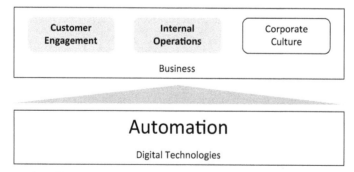

Figure A.4 Business impact of Automation

Let us take an Automation example of a typical Customer PO process.

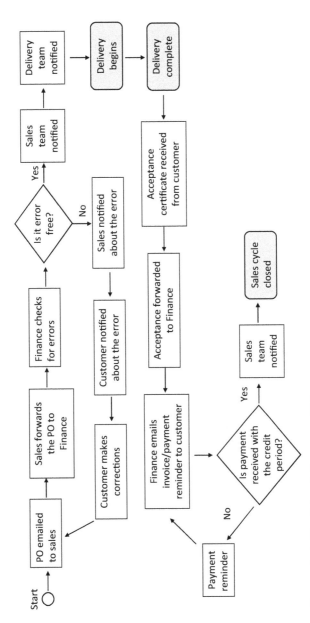

Figure A.5 Traditional Customer PO process

Traditional Process

1. The customer e-mails the PO to the Sales team.
2. The PO is forwarded by the Sales to the Finance team.
3. Finance checks for errors. If there is one, the customer is notified. Customer sends the corrected PO.
4. If no error, then the Sales team is notified accordingly by the Finance.
5. Sales team then notifies the Delivery team and work starts.
6. Once the delivery is complete, customer sends an acceptance certificate which is forwarded to Finance.
7. Finance then sends an invoice to the customer, keeping Sales in the loop.
8. If a customer doesn't pay within the required credit period, a payment reminder is sent to the customer.
9. Once the payment is received, the Sales is notified, and the sales cycle is closed.

Automated Process

1. Customer procurement team e-mails the PO to bot ID, which then triggers automation.
2. It automatically checks for errors and notifies the customer if there is one, keeping the Sales, Finance, and Delivery teams in the loop.
3. If no PO error, the work starts.
4. Once the delivery is complete and delivery acceptance is e-mailed to the bot ID by the customer, the invoicing automation process is triggered.
5. An auto-invoice is e-mailed to the customer, keeping the Sales and Finance team in the loop.
6. If payment is not received within the required credit days, a payment reminder is sent automatically.
7. Once the payment is received, Sales and Finance teams are notified through auto-e-mails, and the sales cycle is closed.

The Automation can achieve cost and lead time reduction by 70 percent.[11]

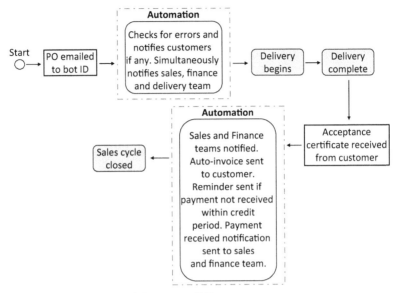

Figure A.6 Automated Customer PO process

Data Science and Data Analytics

Businesses generate massive amounts of data daily. Data is of two types:

- Structured data, which is well organized and has some degree of correlation with each other
- Unstructured data, which is not well organized and is uncorrelated with each other

An example of structured data is an entry in an Excel sheet containing rows and columns featuring similar types of data. An example of unstructured data is the data coming from various sources such as application servers, customer location services, social media, and so on. Most of the business data is unstructured. Such data needs to be collected, extracted, checked, reformatted, aggregated with other data, and filtered. The big challenge for the business is how to manage this data effectively to gain useful insights and take important actions or decisions based on them.

Data Science is an umbrella term that encompasses Data Analytics, Data Mining, Machine Learning, and several other related disciplines. It is the process of gathering both structured and unstructured data from multiple sources of data sets and applying appropriate algorithms to make data ready for analysis. *Data Analytics* is the process of extracting meaningful insights and offering predictions through various visualization techniques applied to business data extracted from various sources.

To understand Data Science and Data Analytics better, let us consider the process of making a smoothie. It requires a recipe, ingredients, and a blender. In the context of Data Science, a recipe can be compared to an algorithm, ingredients to data, and a blender to a tool. Just as a blender mixes all the ingredients as per the quantities stated in the recipe to make a smoothie, similarly the Data Science tool applies the right algorithms to the data to give you the required answer. Suppose you ask a person expert in selling smoothies to give insights on what you could do with the smoothie. He might say, well the temperature is hot close to 35 degrees, and you are thirsty, so you can drink the smoothie. Or you can sell the smoothie to someone for 10 euros. Such types of insights are provided by Data Analytics. You can select the way you want to present the smoothie, either in a glass, in a bottle, or in a plastic cup. This can be compared to Data Visualization which allows you to view data in a certain way.

There are five types of algorithms that are applied to data:

1. *Classification Algorithms.* They ask the question—is this X or Y? For example, should a discount be offered to a customer? Yes or No? This algorithm can be extended from two choices to multiple choices, in which the algorithm will choose the most likely one.
2. *Anomaly Detection Algorithms.* They ask the question- is this different? For example, is the vendor invoice of $50,000 normal, when all the other vendor invoices are usually less than $1000?
3. *Regression Algorithms.* They ask the question—how much or how many? For example, how much will I sell in the third quarter?
4. *Clustering Algorithms.* They ask the question—how is this organized? For example, which customers are likely to buy our products?

5. *Reinforcement Learning Algorithms.* They ask the question—What should I do now? What action or decision should I take now? A reinforcement learning algorithm gathers data it learns from trial and error and provides the user with the most likely solution. For example, now that a customer has asked for a discount, what should I do? Should I offer him a discount of 5 percent or offer no discount at all or give away an additional item free of cost? These algorithms learn from all the past customer interactions and behavior data points and offer the most likely solution.[12]

Data Science and Data Analytics can impact all the business areas of Digital Transformation such as Customer Engagement, Internal Operations, and Corporate Culture.

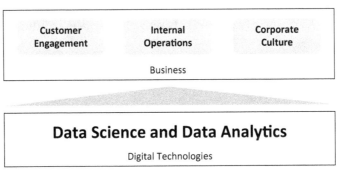

Figure A.7 *Business impact of Data Science and Data Analytics*

Recently, I was working on a strategy consulting project on Data Analytics with a B2C client named ABC Learning (name changed) offering education services to its end users. The objective of the assignment for the client was to achieve customer satisfaction for its end users through Data Analytics. Data Science algorithms were implemented to collect all the data points in the following two areas:

1. Presales
2. Instructor-led live learning courses

These two areas directly impacted the customer experience which in turn had an impact on customer satisfaction. Presales data points included all the interactions from the point of the customer's first visit on ABC Learning's website, and all its interactions with the chatbot until a purchase was made by the customer. Instructor-led live learning data points included online and offline interactions the instructor had with students.

For presales, the following key insights were presented:

- Customers who stay on the website for more than two minutes are more likely to interact with the chatbot.
- Most customers who visit the website after 8 p.m. stay longer than 10 minutes.
- A prospective customer visits the website at least three times with a maximum gap of 48 hours between any two visits.
- Longer a customer interacts with the chatbot, more likely is he/she to trust the bot and eventually purchase a learning course.

For learning, the following key insights were presented:

- Students tend to interact more over the collaboration forums where an instructor responds to their queries within 8 hours.
- Courses where instructors provide lots of interactive case studies and videos which last no longer than 45 minutes get a relatively higher rating.
- For all the students who view the recordings of live courses stored in the archives, the view rate is high after 7 p.m. and within three days of the assignment submission deadline.
- Students who are working professionals are more likely to view recorded videos than live training.

So, with these insights, the following recommendations were made:

1. Train the bots to remain engaged with prospective customers through e-mails, WhatsApp, and text messages, even after they leave the website.

2. Discontinue instructor-led live learning sessions and introduce self-paced interactive learning through pre-recorded instructor videos and continuous support.

These changes were implemented by ABC Learning within 12 weeks, and customer satisfaction was improved by 25 percent.

Blockchain

A *Blockchain* is a chain of blocks that contain information. This technology gained popularity when it was adopted to create a digital cryptocurrency—Bitcoin. Each block contains three elements:

- Data
- Hash
- Hash of previous block

Data can be any information or a transactional entry. A *hash* is a unique identity assigned to the block, and *hash of previous block* effectively creates the chain of blocks. Hence the term "Blockchain."

Blockchain works on the following principles:

1. Distributed database: Each party on the blockchain has access to the entire blockchain and its complete history. There is no single party controlling the blocks, for example, all five users in Figure A.9 have access to the entire database.

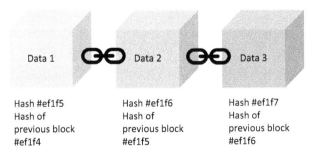

Figure A.8 Elements of Blockchain

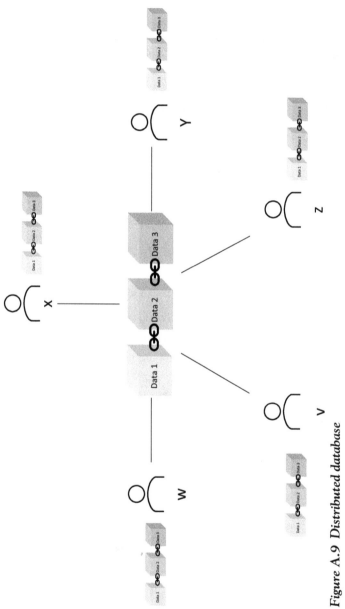

Figure A.9 Distributed database

2. Peer-to-peer communications: Transactions happen between the peers instead of a central node.

3. Transparency: Each transaction is visible to anyone on the system and each party can verify it directly without an intermediary. This creates trust between the users. For example, user X wants to send a confirmation receipt of $500 to user Y and does not want other users to see this information. User X must turn on the privacy settings to keep the data private and confidential. This transaction is recorded as an additional block and shared with all the users on the network. They would only see a new block added to the blockchain with a time stamp and a hash but cannot see the data in that block.

4. Irreversibility of records: Once the transaction has been made, the data in the block cannot be altered or the block cannot be deleted. A new block needs to be added in the end explaining the changes and it is distributed to all the users on the network.

5. Automation: Users can set algorithms or create rules that allow automatic transactions between them.

As shown in Figure A.14, Blockchain has a strong impact on Internal Operations.

Within the scope of Internal Operations, blockchain can impact all functional areas. However, we will discuss business impact on Sales, Marketing, Finance, Supply, and HR, which are predicted to be the most impacted.

In Sales, blockchain can track all the details about the customer and save valuable due diligence time. Some customers may license their private and confidential data to businesses in exchange for licensing fees. Due to the data cryptography, security, and transparency provided by blockchain, customers can trust businesses better. The intermediaries such as a bank or a notary will be eliminated. This can save transactional costs for both the firm and its customers.

In Marketing, blockchain would enable firms to do peer-to-peer communications with their customers, which would enable the firms to market their brands to the right audience.

In HR, with blockchain, it would be easier to run background or verification checks and track the work history of an employee, which

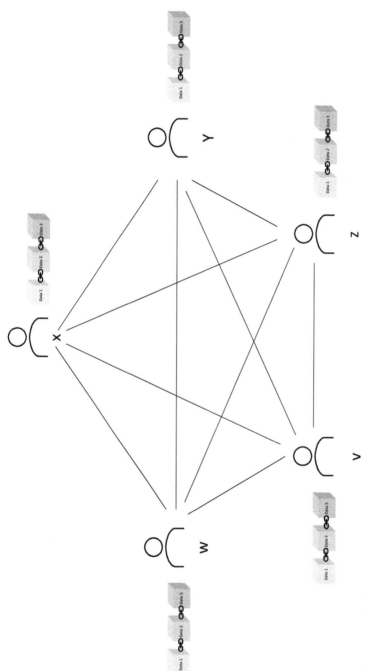

Figure A.10 Peer-to-peer communications

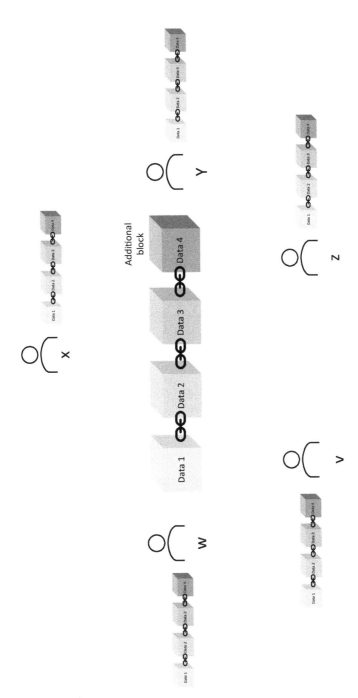

Figure A.11 Transparency

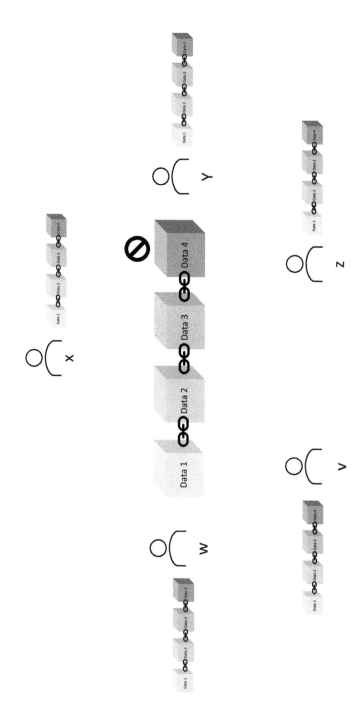

Figure A.12 Irreversibility of records

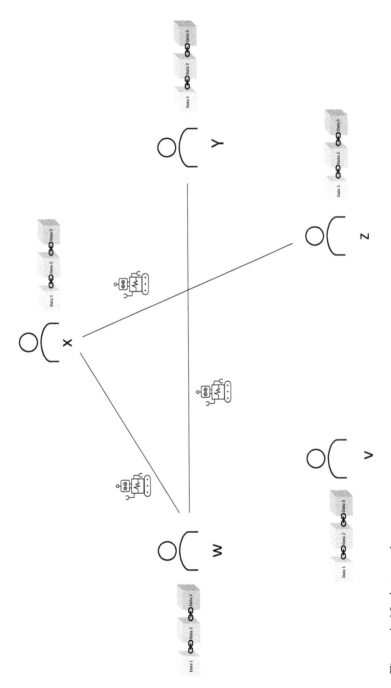

Figure A.13 Automation

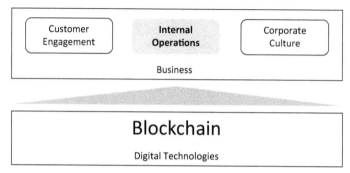

Figure A.14 Business impact of Blockchain

is mandatory by law in some countries. It will improve the chances of finding the right candidate for the job.

Blockchain would impact the supply chains too. Currently, it is very challenging for big firms to procure through various partners and keep track of each transaction. With a digital ledger offered by blockchain, it will be easier to track each of the partner transactions. Blockchain will improve the inventory audit process where all the finest details about inventory procurement can be tracked. Contracts can be stored digitally which can add trust among the buyers and sellers and eliminate the need for an intermediary.

In Finance, blockchain would change how people can search for financial data, both public and private, for a company right from its incorporation till date.[13]

Internet of Things (IoT)

The Internet of Things or IoT is the network of physical devices, vehicles, home appliances, and other items embedded with electronics, software, sensors, actuators, and connectivity, which enables these objects to connect and exchange data. The global IoT market size in terms of revenue is expected to reach $650 billion by 2026.[14] Figure A.15 shows the IoT value chain.

The global IoT spending is forecasted to be $1.1 trillion by 2023,[15] out of which approximately 30 percent is estimated to be spent on services, 25 percent on apps, 25 percent on platforms, 10 percent on connectivity, and 10 percent on chipsets and sensors.

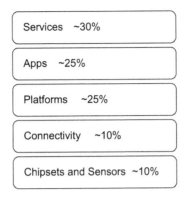

Figure A.15 IoT value chain

Let us consider an IoT use case: Smart Metering solution as shown in Figure A.16. Data is transmitted by the IoT-enabled smart meters through either 4G or 5G networks to a datacenter where it is collected and processed by a cloud-based platform. Users can then subscribe to the service which allows them to check utility usage on a smartphone remotely in real time. The application can also offer users an energy savings percentile score showing how much better has it performed compared to other users.

Figure A.16 Smart Metering solution

As shown in Figure A.17, IoT mainly impacts the business area Internal Operations among which Development unit, Product/Service Delivery, and Supply/Logistics have the maximum impact.

IoT combined with AI has enabled a new revolution in industrial manufacturing called Industry 4.0. First Industrial Revolution or *Industry 1.0*, involved mechanization through water and steam power. The

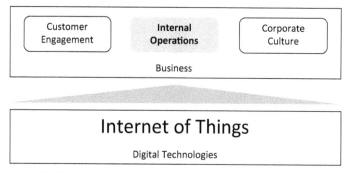

Figure A.17 Business impact of IoT

second Industrial Revolution or *Industry 2.0,* involved mass production and assembly lines using electricity. The third Industrial Revolution or *Industry 3.0,* involved the adoption of software enabling automation, and the fourth Industrial Revolution, or *Industry 4.0,* includes smart and autonomous systems fueled by the latest digital emerging technologies such as AI, IoT, Data, and Digital Twins.

5G

5G is a wireless cellular technology offering connectivity for user applications to run on different devices. It offers speeds as high as 10 Gbps, low latency, operational flexibility, and energy efficiency based on specific use cases that can be carried over any suitable network. As compared to the previous technologies, 5G supports:

- 10 to 100 times more user data
- 1000 times more data volumes
- 5 times improved latency
- 100 times smaller devices
- low operational costs
- 5 times improved network energy efficiency
- 3 times spectral efficiency
- devices with battery life more than 10 years
- a common network offering various 5G use cases[16]

5G use cases can vary as per different user demands and different running applications. For example, a high-speed autonomous car is a mission-critical use case that cannot afford to have transmission delays. Whereas a sensor monitoring operations in agricultural land, which requires reporting the readings at regular intervals may not need to be time critical. These different use cases are handled by one core network using a functionality known as Network Slicing. It simply means slicing the network into parts, so that each user or an application gets its slice as per its requirements. It enables you to build multiple logical networks known as network slices on top of a common shared physical infrastructure. These network slices, typically one for each kind of service, are separate and independent to the extent that if something goes wrong in one slice, it will not affect the other slices. This separation and independence also enable the user to add new slices without impacting the rest of the network.

5G use cases can be broadly classified into the following categories:

- Enhanced Mobile Broadband
- Massive IoT
- Critical IoT
- Industry Specific
- Fixed Wireless Access (FWA)[17]

Enhanced Mobile Broadband provides large volumes of data transfer, higher data rates, and lower latencies on best effort while enabling additional capabilities such as extended device battery life, extended coverage, and uplink heavy data rates. Typical applications are wearables, drones, online gaming, cameras, and sensors.

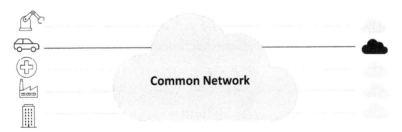

Figure A.18 Network Slicing

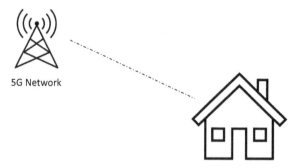

5G Network

Figure A.19 Fixed Wireless Access

Massive IoT or massive machine-type communication is designed to provide a wide area coverage and deep penetration for hundreds of thousands of devices per square kilometer. Its main objective is to provide ubiquitous connectivity with relatively low software and hardware complexity and low energy operation. Many of these devices supported are battery powered or driven by alternative energy supplies and have small payloads. Examples include transport and logistics, smart agriculture, environment, industrial utilities, smart cities, smart buildings, and consumer devices. *Critical IoT*, also known as critical machine type communication, or ultra-reliable low latency communications is for time-critical communications. It can deliver data within strict latency bounds with the required guaranteed levels even in heavily loaded networks. Examples include intelligent transport systems, smart utilities, remote healthcare, smart manufacturing, and fully immersive AR/VR.

Industry Specific use cases focus on verticals such as automotive, utilities, healthcare, mining, transport, and so on.

FWA is a wireless solution where customers subscribe to services that complement fixed services such as fiber, cable, or x-DSL. As shown in Figure A.19, the user in the home gets the Internet, voice, video on demand, and connected home services through a high-speed outdoor 5G network.

Cloud

We shall understand the two concepts: Cloud Computing and Virtualization. Consider a company selling online products to customers globally. It has a datacenter in London comprising 100 physical servers. To run such a setup, it requires physical space, storage, cooling system, cabling technicians, electricity, and power backup. Each server requires 4 GB RAM memory, 2 CPUs, and 50 GB hard disk space for storage. So total resources required are 400 GB RAM memory, 200 CPUs, and 5 TB of hard disk space to run such a datacenter. The company incurs daily operational costs. Imagine it is Christmas time, and the number of people visiting and shopping on the website increases 10 times. So, to manage this increased load, the company needs 50 more servers now. If the company decides to buy 50 more servers, the total servers will be 150, and the total resources required to run 150 servers become 600 GB RAM memory, 300 CPUs, and 7.5 TB of hard disk space. But after Christmas is over, the number of people visiting the website reduces and the requirement again becomes 100 servers. Thus 200 GB RAM (600–400 GB), 100 CPUs (300–200 CPUs), and 2.5 TB (7.5–5 TB) hard disk space will be wasted. To solve this problem, the company decided to hire a cloud consultant who offered them a courageous solution:

Sell off all the datacenter assets and go to Amazon Web Services (AWS). After you open an account with them, you can buy the resources that you need (400 GB of RAM, 200 CPUs, and 5 TB of hard disk space) online. During Christmas time, you just pay for the additional resources you need, and after Christmas is over, you can give back the resources to AWS. Suppose your business goes down and you need a smaller number of resources, then you only pay for as much as you need.

This concept of online on-demand delivery of resources such as memory, CPU, and storage based on a pay-as-you-go pricing model is known as *Cloud Computing*.

Now let us try to understand how the concept of virtualization works.

Consider a physical server with the following resources: 16GB RAM, 8 CPUs, and 500 GB storage space. A virtualization software known as *hypervisor* needs to be added on top of the physical hardware or server to create several virtual machines (VM) as per one's requirement. As shown in Figure A.20, 5 VMs have been created each of 2 GB RAM, 1 CPU, and 50 GB of hard disk. This concept of moving from physical resources to logical ones is known as *Virtualization*.

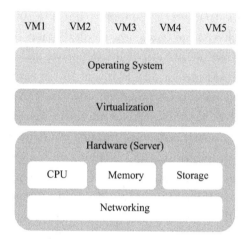

Figure A.20 Virtualization

There are three types of services provided by the cloud, which are known as XaaS or Anything(X)-as-a-service. These three services are Infrastructure-as-a-Service or Iaas, Platform-as-a-Service or PaaS, and Software-as-a-Service or SaaS.

Let us try to understand the Cloud service model shown in Figure A.21. It consists of several layers as shown.

The first one is hardware or a physical server, which comprises resources such as memory, CPU, storage, and networking. The next one is virtualization, which is enabled through hypervisors. The above layer is the operating system. After that comes the middleware, then comes runtime, then data, and the last one is the application layer or simply apps. Suppose a firm buys a service from AWS, where all the layers from hardware to operating system or OS are to be managed by AWS, and the remaining layers are to be managed by the firm, it is IaaS. If it buys services, where all the layers until runtime are managed by AWS and the remaining layers such as data and application, are to be managed by the firm, it is PaaS. And if it buys a service, where all the layers from hardware to apps are managed by AWS, it is SaaS.

There are three types of cloud deployment models:

- Public cloud
- Private cloud
- Hybrid cloud

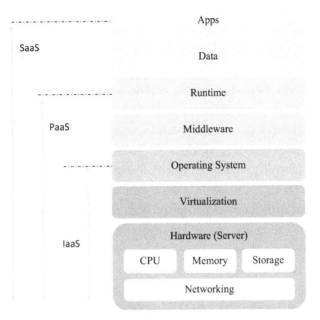

Figure A.21 Cloud service model

Public cloud providers such as AWS, Microsoft Azure, and Google Cloud known as hyperscalers provide different types of services such as IaaS, PaaS, and SaaS. The private cloud is also known as enterprise cloud or on-premises cloud. If an enterprise doesn't want to use the public cloud due to some security reasons, they can go with the option of private cloud. In a private cloud, it can virtualize its IT resources within its own datacenter and run the required applications. The hybrid cloud is a combination of both public and private clouds. Normally, in a hybrid cloud solution, resources such as memory or CPU are virtualized in its own datacenter, whereas a public cloud is used for resources such as storage or database. Most of the enterprises today prefer the hybrid cloud model.

The benefits of cloud computing are:

- First, the shift from CAPEX to OPEX. One no longer needs to make heavy capital investments in datacenter, IT resources, or physical servers. One can sign up for OPEX based pay-as-you-go pricing model.
- Second, one can save datacenter maintenance costs.

- Third, one no longer needs to guess the capacity required by the infrastructure. If there is an increase in demand, one can simply scale out resources and when the demand reduces, just scale in them.
- Fourth, massive economies of scale. One can benefit from massive economies of scale with higher volumes and lower pay-as-you-go pricing models.
- Fifth, increased speed and agility. New resources can be deployed fast when the load or demand on resources increases.
- And sixth, global deployment. With the help of cloud computing, one can deploy applications to the customers anywhere across the globe.

Imagine you run a business that has a datacenter at a certain location. The biggest risk that you would carry as a business is that some events happen or disasters strike the building where datacenter is located. The hyperscalers address this problem by building a large group of datacenters known as *Regions*. The regions can be across any location across the globe such as Mumbai, London, Paris, New York, and so on. In a region, multiple datacenters provide compute, storage, and other services that help to run your applications. Each region can be connected to another region through a high-speed fiber network.

Regions are divided into *Availability Zones*. An availability zone is a single datacenter or group of datacenters within the region. Availability zones are located tens of miles apart from each other. This is close enough

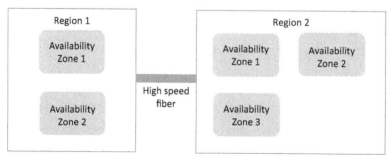

Figure A.22 Regions and Availability Zones

to have low latency between availability zones. If disaster strikes one part of the region, they are distant enough to reduce the chances of multiple availability zones getting affected.

Gamification

In a business context, Gamification is defined as the application of game design principles to change organizational behavior, processes, or ways of working. It has the potential to make a good impact on all three business areas: Customer Engagement, Internal Operations, and Corporate Culture as shown in Figure A.23. Both employees and customers can be engaged through Gamification.

Freshdesk is a good example of the engagement of employees through Gamification. It provided a helpdesk software program for the customer support center. The help desk employees often did monotonous routine work and were loaded, demotivated, and over-stressed. This was changed into fun by Gamification, by treating the customer inquiries or tickets into gaming tasks or challenges and were distributed to employees, who were rewarded points and batches for solving the queries. There were different achievement rewards such as "first call resolution" and "fast resolution" focused on making the customers happy. The employee performances were tracked on a leaderboard. There were rewards and recognition given to them such as "employee of the month."[18]

There was a tutoring company based in India that created a gamified experience for students (customers) enrolled in its courses for solving

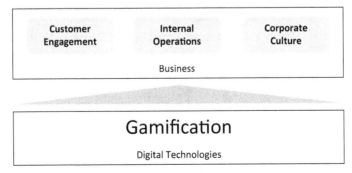

Figure A.23 Business impact of Gamification

homework assignments. It was observed that completing and submitting the weekly assignments was quite a monotonous and boring job for the students. So, the students were enrolled in a game that included all the weekly assignments. The assignments were self-adaptive which means that the difficulty level was to be adjusted depending on the performance of the students. Points were awarded to those who finished the assignments accurately. Some assignments needed students to be teamed up. There were some additional bonus points given out to those who finished the assignment fast. A weekly leaderboard would show the standings of each of them. The student who finished at the top of the leader board was the winner and received a business book as the winning prize.

Extended Reality (XR)

The Extended Reality (XR) is a broad technology that comprises Virtual Reality (VR), Augmented Reality (AR), and Mixed Reality (MR). In *VR*, a total simulated three-dimensional experience is generated for the users using computer-generated graphics to provide an immersive experience of the virtual world. In *AR*, digital elements such as text, graphics, and video streams are added or augmented to the real world. *MR* is an in-between hybrid stage where the real-world environment merges with a computer-generated virtual one. Either you can add virtual objects to the real experiences as in AR or bring in real objects to your virtual experiences as in VR.

Along with VR, there is a headset associated, which a user is supposed to wear over the eyes. Being opaque, a user cannot see the outside world through it. Users can see only the computer-generated virtual images generated by the headset, through the lens covering the eyes. There are two types of VR headsets: standalone and tethered. A standalone VR headset has built-in software that generates virtual images. A tethered VR headset needs to be connected through a cable, to the external device such as a PC which runs the software that generates the virtual images. A standalone device is more portable, less expensive, and easy to set up. However, the resolution, image quality, and immersive experience as compared to a tethered one are low. A tethered device provides a better quality of immersive experience and higher image resolution than a standalone one. However, it is a bit more complicated to set up, not easily portable, and more expensive than standalone. Both standalone and tethered devices contain multiple sensors to continuously calculate the orientation of the user's head. So, whenever the user moves up and down, turns sideways, or back and forth, it will recalculate the view of what a user is seeing and send slightly different views to each eye, to generate an immersive 3D experience.

Many AR devices use mobile phones and tablets with cameras that can show a real-time image of the real world and generate overlays of virtual objects over them. These virtual objects can appear as if they are a part of the real world. These virtual objects can be anywhere in the real space and reposition themselves as we move around in the real space. Some of the retail sites such as IKEA use AR, which allows the users to add the product in their real space. For example, a user can check how IKEA furniture looks in the living room or bedroom using the AR app. People generally prefer quick, casual AR use cases on the devices they usually have, unlike VR. However, there are some head-worn AR products available too.

MR can be viewed as a spectrum between AR and VR, as an in-between hybrid space between them. The objects can be classified as real/virtual and interactive/noninteractive. Real objects are digital copies of the ones that exist in the real space. Virtual objects are generated through computer simulations and don't exist in real space. Interactive objects are both real and virtual ones such as text, images, and videos that users can move, resize, and rotate in virtual space. Noninteractive objects are both real and virtual ones such as text, image, and videos that the user cannot move, resize, or rotate in virtual space. As shown in Figure A.24, when you start adding real and noninteractive objects to VR or virtual and noninteractive objects to AR, you move toward the MR. When the real and virtual objects are interactive, it becomes a full MR experience.

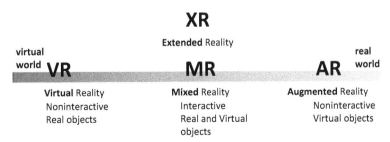

Figure A.24 Extended Reality (XR) spectrum

Metaverse

There has been lots of buzz and hype around Metaverse. It was first coined by Neal Stephenson in his science fiction novel Snow Crash in 1992. It was a virtual reality space where people interacted using their avatars. It became more popular when Facebook announced its commitment to develop Metaverse and changed its name to Meta. Then Microsoft announced its investments in Metaverse. Now, it has been a focus of the business community on how Metaverse could change work.

Metaverse is a combination of many real-world technologies such as virtual and augmented reality, blockchain, cloud computing, AI, computer–human interaction, advanced simulations and graphics designs, and high-speed Internet connectivity. It is a shared 3D virtual world space, where you can purchase and monetize real estate, create scenarios, games, and other VR experiences, express yourself through customizable avatars, meet and collaborate with remote colleagues, socialize and make new friends, shop for real and virtual products, attend concerts, trade shows and learning events, play virtual reality games, sell in-game assets for cryptocurrency tokens, invest in digital artwork through nonfungible tokens (NFT), get a job, brainstorm and design products in 3D, and many more.[19]

Nike launched several initiatives to set foot in the Metaverse. Nike entered a partnership with Fortnite, an online gaming brand, where two characters in a game developed by Fortnite were wearing Nike's digital sneakers, called skins. Nike developed blockchain-compatible sneakers called CryptoKicks. Those who bought a pair of CryptoKicks received a digital asset attached to the shoe's unique identifier. When the shoes were sold to someone else, ownership was transferred by trading the digital shoes and any related digital assets stored in a digital locker, a cryptocurrency wallet-type app. If anyone on Nike had been playing CryptoKitties, as an owner of CrytoKicks, they would be able to breed the digital shoe with another digital shoe to create the "shoe offspring"—an entirely new shoe design. Nike in partnership with Roblox, created a virtual world called Nikeland on Roblox. Participants could use Nike-branded shoes and apparel to dress up their avatars, check out product offerings, and try new products. Nike wanted to observe and test which products appealed to a younger audience. If kids showed a desire for Nike shoes and apparel in the Metaverse, the company would produce the same in the real world. In late 2021, Nike filed to protect seven trademarks in the Metaverse, signaling the company's intention to make and sell virtual sneakers and clothes. These included its name, like the Nike swoosh logo, the "Just Do it" slogan, and the Air Jordan and "Jumpman" logos. In December 2021, Nike announced that it was acquiring RTFKT, a leading brand that designed digital sneakers and next-generation collectibles that blended culture and gaming. Nike CEO Donahoe said that it provided an opportunity to serve athletes and creators at the intersection of sport, creativity, gaming, and culture.

However, Nike's competitor Adidas took a community-first approach that focused on partnerships with newer Metaverse platforms and the creation of NFTs. An NFT is a nonfungible token, a unique unit of data stored on a blockchain, which is a form of digital ledger. NFTs could be owned and thus bought and sold. An NFT could be in the form of a photo, visual art, audio and video-even an in-game digital parcel of land. Unlike bitcoins, which were fungible and interchangeable, each NFT was unique and thus not interchangeable. Adidas released a series of NFTs that gave owners access to special physical goods such as hoodies, and to future digital experiences. Adidas purchased a Bored Apes Yatch Club NFT#8774 in September 2021. It also purchased land in The Sandbox to create AdiVerse to rival Nikeland on Roblox. Players could use the NFTs as virtual tokens to purchase virtual merchandize and dress up their avatars in the Metaverse.[20] How to monetize in the Metaverse? It is an interesting business challenge to solve.

Summary

- AI platform consists of four main building blocks:
  1. Machine Learning
  2. Natural Language Processing (NLP)
  3. Machine Vision
  4. Large Language Models (LLM)
- There are seven business-critical capabilities of AI:
  1. Pattern Recognition
  2. Prediction
  3. Classification

4. Facial Recognition

5. Speech to Text/ Text to Speech

6. Personalization

7. Generative AI

- There are two kinds of Automation: Rule-based Automation and AI-driven automation.
- Rule-based Automation is further classified into RPA and RBA.
- There are five types of Data Science algorithms: Classification, Anomaly Detection, Regression, Clustering, Reinforcement Learning.
- Blockchain is based on the following principles: Distributed database, Peer-to-peer communications, Transparency, Irreversibility of records, and Automation.
- IoT value chain comprises Services, Apps, Platforms, Connectivity, and Chips and Sensors.
- 5G use cases are classified into Enhanced Mobile Broadband, Massive IoT, Critical IoT, Industry Specific, and Fixed Wireless Access (FWA).
- There are three types of cloud deployment models: Public cloud, Private cloud, and Hybrid cloud.
- There are three types of cloud services: SaaS, PaaS, and IaaS.
- The Extended Reality (XR) is a broad technology that comprises Virtual Reality (VR), Augmented Reality (AR), and Mixed Reality (MR).
- Either you can add virtual objects to the real experiences as in AR or bring in real objects to your virtual experiences as in VR.
- Metaverse is a combination of many real-world technologies such as VR, AR, blockchain, cloud computing, AI, computer-human interaction, advanced simulations and graphics designs, and high-speed Internet connectivity.

Conclusion

An important question is "When is the right time to implement Digital Strategy Framework?"

Most of the incumbents have already begun with Digital Transformation. Does it mean that they should stop their current work, redo the strategy, and restart the transformation? No. Those who don't have a clear and concrete Digital Strategy should consider applying this entire framework immediately. It can make their Digital Transformation more focused and easier to implement. Those who have a Digital Strategy should review if they have missed out on any important steps described in this framework. They should consider using this entire framework at their next major strategy review or next phase of the current strategy.

The Delivery phase of Strategy Execution is a time-bound activity. The Strategic Priorities should be continuously reviewed based on the feedback from different stakeholders in the Delivery phase. Your firm can plan the exit once the Wanted Position is achieved, and the Strategic Priorities are met.

Most of the tasks or activities you execute while implementing the framework would be something you have never done before. Hence, I would suggest the readers to document the best practices, lessons learnt, what worked, and what didn't work and share it with the rest of the organization.

The Digital Strategy Framework can produce the best results when customized and applied as per your business needs. The fictitious case study presented in Chapter 6 must have provided you with some implementation ideas.

Currently, we are living in the times where Generative AI or simply GenAI, a new digital transformation technology, has created lots of hype in the market, since the release of ChatGPT, an AI-powered chatbot by OpenAI. Incumbent businesses are trying to understand how to implement and seek value from it. My advice to the business incumbents: Do not rush through the GenAI deployment without a strategy in place. Make best use of the Digital Strategy Framework in this book to either develop a new strategy or revise your existing one for GenAI.

Although the case study is fictitious, the names given to the characters are the names of real people. They are my ex-colleagues who have helped me grow professionally and with whom I have had a great time.

If you have any questions or feedback about the book, connect with me through LinkedIn:

www.linkedin.com/in/amit-prabhu26

Or through my website:

www.amitprabhu.net

Hope you have enjoyed reading the book, as much as I have enjoyed writing it. Remember, this book is not just about Information...It's all about *Transformation*!

Notes

Introduction

1. McKinsey (2019).
2. Venkatraman (2017).

Chapter 1

1. Tvasta (2023).
2. Segran (2018).
3. Wikipedia (2023a).
4. Ibid.
5. Coles and Edelman (2011), pp. 2–3.
6. Torres (2019).
7. Sull, Turconi, and Zanjani (2022).
8. Collis, Shaffer, and Hartman (2016), p. 1.
9. Casadesus-Masanell and Kim (2015), p. 13.
10. Ibid.
11. Brand Minds (2018).
12. Ibid.
13. McKinnon (2023).
14. Ibid.
15. World Economic Forum (2023a).
16. Donovan and Benko (2016). Reprinted with permission from "AT&T's Talent Overhaul."
17. Training Industry (2023).
18. Digiculum (2023).
19. Pelow and Austin (2019). Reprinted with Permission.

Chapter 2

1. Casadesus-Masanell (2014), p. 5.
2. Maverick and Reviewed by Brown (2022).
3. Abbosh, Savic, and Moore. (2018), p. 3.

4. *The Wall Street Journal* (2023).

5. Kenton (2023).

6. Uduu and Kareem (2022).

7. CFI Team (2023).

8. Uduu and Kareem (2022).

9. Collis, Shaffer, and Hartman (2016), p. 1.

10. Prabhu (2020).

11. *Share Now Website* (2023).

12. Porter and Heppelmann (2014), p. 8.

13. Venkatraman (2017).

14. Fader, Hardie, and Ross (2022), p. 3.

15. Shapiro (2013), p. 3.

16. Pluralsight (2023).

17. Niessing, Henry, and Peters (2018).

Chapter 3

1. Oh and Myer (2016). Reprinted with Permission.

Chapter 4

1. Sinha, Sahay, Shastri, and Lorimer (2022).

2. Auto Pilot Review (2023).

3. Autocrypt (2023).

4. Van Alstyne, Parker and Choudary (2016), p. 5.

5. Bianchi (2023).

6. Dixon (2023).

7. de Jong and Vermeulen (2022). Reprinted with Permission.

8. www.digiculum.com/.

9. Catlin, Deetjen, Lorenz, Nandan, and Sharma (2023).

10. Pidun, Reeves, and Schüssler (2019).

11. Mediacorp (2023b).

12. Ibid.

13. Wattpad.com (2023).

14. Mediacorp (2023a).

15. Mediacorp.sg (2023).

16. Digiculum.com (2023).

17. Blog by Sisense team (2023).

Chapter 5

 1. Tarver, reviewed by Brock, fast checked by Rathburn (2022).

 2. werbackspace.com (2023).

 3. Statista.com (2023).

 4. Nikkei Asia (2017).

 5. Rao and Speculand (2021).

 6. DBS.com (2023a).

 7. Marketing-Interactive (2018).

 8. Rao and Speculand (2021).

 9. Gupta and Davin (2019), p. 23.

10. Wikipedia (2023c).

11. Gupta and Davin (2019), p. 41.

12. Prabhu (2018).

13. Braineet (2023).

14. Marketsandmarkets (2023).

15. World Economic Forum (2023).

16. Wikipedia (2023b).

17. YouTube Video (2022).

18. Hui (2017).

19. www.dbs.com/livemore/sparks/index.html.

20. https://shortyawards.com/11th/dbs-sparks-mini-series.

21. DBS.com (2023b).

22. DBS.com (2023c).

23. DBS.com (2023d).

24. DBS.com (2023e).

25. Rao and Speculand (2021).

26. Ibid.

27. Koh, Speculand, and Wong (2020), pp. 5–6.

28. Rao and Speculand (2021).

29. Jouany and Makipaa (2023).

30. Prabhu (2018).

31. *CEO Today* (2023).

32. Rao and Speculand (2021).

33. Innosight (2023).

34. Rao and Speculand (2021).

35. *CEO Today* (2023).

36. Ibid.

37. DBS.com (2023f).

38. "DBS Bank. Live more, Bank Less" (2020).

39. DBS.com (2023g).

40. Koh, Speculand, and Wong (2020).

Chapter 6

1. Restrepo and Ojomo (2022).

Appendix

1. Eliacik (2023).

2. Ransbotham, Kiron, Gerbert, and Reeves (2017), p. 8.

3. Ibid.

4. Kirvela and Lundmark (2018).

5. Prabhu (2018).

6. Dawar (May–June 2018). Republished by permission.

7. Prabhu (2018).

8. Ibid.

9. Ibid.

10. Ibid.

11. Ibid.

12. Ibid.

13. Ibid.

14. Marketsandmarkets.com (2023).

15. Howarth (2023).

16. Prabhu (2020).

17. Ericsson (2023).

18. YouTube Video (2012).

19. XR Today (2022).

20. Sawhney and Goodman (2022).

References

"DBS Bank. Live more, Bank Less." October 29, 2020. https://medium.com/@DBSBank/the-importance-of-being-a-failure-bf503c5f7afa.

Abbosh, O., V. Savic, and M. Moore. January 29, 2018. "How Likely Is Your Industry to Be Disrupted? This 2x2 Matric Will Tell You." *Harvard Business Review*, p. 3.

Auto Pilot Review. 2023. "SAE Self-Driving Levels 0 to 5 for Automation—What They Mean." www.autopilotreview.com/self-driving-cars-sae-levels/ (accessed April 24, 2023).

Autocrypt. January 13, 2023. "The State of Level 3 Autonomous Driving in 2023: Ready for the Mass Market?" https://autocrypt.io/the-state-of-level-3-autonomous-driving-in-2023/#:~:text=The%20State%20of%20Level%203%20Autonomous%20Driving%20in%202023%20%7C%20AUTOCRYPT.

Bianchi, T. February 24, 2023. *Statista*. www.statista.com/statistics/266249/advertising-revenue-of-google/.

Blog by Sisense team. 2023. www.sisense.com/blog/scorecard-vs-dashboard-adds-business-intelligence/ (accessed April 24, 2023).

Braineet. 2023. "My Starbucks Idea: An Open Innovation Case-Study." www.braineet.com/blog/my-starbucks-idea-case-study#toc-0 (accessed April 24, 2023).

Brand Minds. December 14, 2018. "Why Did Kodak Fail and What Can You Learn From Its Demise?" https://brand-minds.medium.com/why-did-kodak-fail-and-what-can-you-learn-from-its-failure-70b92793493c (accessed April 24, 2023).

Casadesus-Masanell, R. and H. Kim. Revised September 8, 2015. "Coursera." *Harvard Business School*, p. 13.

Casadesus-Masanell, R. January 31, 2014. *Industry Analysis. Core curriculum: Strategy*, p. 5. Harvard Business Publishing.

Catlin, T., U. Deetjen, J.T. Lorenz, J. Nandan, and S. Sharma. 2023. "Ecosystems and Platforms: How Insurers Can Turn Vision Into Reality." www.mckinsey.com/industries/financial-services/our-insights/ecosystems-and-platforms-how-insurers-can-turn-vision-into-reality (accessed April 24, 2023).

CEO Today. 2023. "How to Succeed in Digital Transformation When All Around Are Failing." www.ceotodaymagazine.com/2021/06/how-to-succeed-indigital-transformation-when-all-around-are-failing/ (accessed April 24, 2023).

CFI Team. Updated April 3, 2023. "Giffen Good." https://corporatefinanceinstitute.com/resources/economics/giffen-good/.

Coles, P.A. and B. Edelman. November 18, 2011. Revised October 16, 2014. "Attack of the Clones: Birchbox Defends Against Copycat Competitors." *Harvard Business School*, pp. 2–3.

Collis, D., M. Shaffer, and A. Hartman. Revised June 6, 2016. "edX: Strategies for Higher Education." *Harvard Business School*, p. 1.

Dawar, N. May–June 2018. "Marketing in the Age of Alexa." [product# R1803E]. *Harvard Business Review*. Republished by permission.

DBS.com. 2023a. www.dbs.com/about-us/who-we-are/our-vision#:~:text=Making%20Banking%20Joyful,contextual%20banking%20solutions%20and%20experiences (accessed April 24, 2023).

DBS.com. 2023b. www.dbs.com.sg/personal/deposits/pay-with-ease/dbs-paylah# (accessed April 24, 2023).

DBS.com. 2023c. www.dbs.com.sg/personal/landing/new-iwealth/index.html?cid=sg-dbs-vanity-others-new-iwealth (accessed April 24, 2023).

DBS.com. 2023d. www.dbs.com/newsroom/DBS_launches_worlds_first_online_simulation_tool_Treasury_Prism (accessed April 24, 2023).

DBS.com. 2023e. www.dbs.com.sg/personal/marketplace/property/plan (accessed April 24, 2023).

DBS.com. 2023f. www.dbs.com/media/our-position-perspectives.page (accessed April 24, 2023).

DBS.com. 2023g. www.dbs.com/annualreports/2018/downloads/FA_DBS_AR18_26-31-our-2018-priorities.pdf (accessed April 24, 2023).

de Jong, R. and F. Vermeulen. July 2022. "The Strategic Transformation of Royal Philips." London Business School. Reprinted with Permission.

Digiculum.com. 2023. "Creating a Learning Experience." www.digiculum.com/creating-a-learning-experience (accessed April 24, 2023).

Digiculum.com. 2023. www.digiculum.com/evaluating-business-impact (accessed April 24, 2023).

Dixon, S. April 19, 2023. *Statista*. www.statista.com/statistics/268604/annual-revenue-of-facebook/.

Donovan, J. and C. Benko. October 2016. "AT&T's Talent Overhaul." *Harvard Business Review*. Reprinted with permission.

Eliacik, E. January 5, 2023. "Early Bird Benefits in AI Adoption Are About to End." https://dataconomy.com/2023/01/03/ai-adoption-artificial-intelligence-stats/#What_is_AI_adoption?utm_content=cmp-true.

Ericsson. 2023. "A Guide to 5G Network Security 2.0." www.ericsson.com/en/security/a-guide-to-5g-network-security (accessed April 24, 2023).

Fader, P., B.G.S. Hardie, and M. Ross. December 23, 2022. "Do You Really Understand Your Best (and Worst) Customers?" *Harvard Business Review*, p. 3.

Gupta, S. and J. Davin. Revised December 19, 2019. "Digital Marketing." *Core Curriculum: Marketing*, p. 23, 41. Harvard Business Publishing.

Howarth, J. March 16, 2023. "80+ Amazing IoT Statistics (2023–2030)" https://explodingtopics.com/blog/iot-stats.

https://shortyawards.com/11th/dbs-sparks-mini-series.

Hui, C.S., CFO. November, 17, 2017. "Creating Shareholder Value From Digitalization." Powerpoint. www.dbs.com/investorday/presentations/Creating_shareholder_value_from_digitalisation.pdf.

Innosight. 2023. "How DBS Transformed Its Culture to Become the World's Best Bank." www.innosight.com/client_impact_story/dbs-bank/ (accessed April 24, 2023).

Jouany, V. and M. Makipaa. January 01, 2023. "8 Employee Engagement Statistics You Need to Know in 2023." https://haiilo.com/blog/employee-engagement-8-statistics-you-need-to-know/#:~:text=85%25%20of%20Employees%20Are%20Not,are%20engaged%20in%20the%20workplace.

Kenton, W., Reviewed by D. Kindness, Fast checked by S. Kvilhaug. February 26, 2023. "Barriers to Exit: Examples, Tax Implications and Overview."www.investopedia.com/terms/b/barriers-to-exit.asp#:~:text=High%20barriers%20to%20exit%20might,can%20only%20perform%20specific%20tasks.

Kirvela, S. and A. Lundmark. November 6, 2018. "Think Big, Start Small, Scale Fast." www.bcg.com/publications/2018/think-big-start-small-scale-fast-ai-artificial-intelligence-success-recipe-nordic.

Koh, A., R. Speculand, and A. Wong. June 15, 2020. *DBS: Digital Transformation to Best Bank in the World*, pp. 5–6. Singapore Management University.

Marketing-Interactive. May 15, 2018. "DBS Bank Drops 'Living, Breathing Asia' Tagline in SG$30 m Rebrand." www.marketing-interactive.com/dbs-bank-changes-living-breathing-asia-tagline-to-signal-digital-evolution.

Marketsandmarkets. May 2023. "Chatbot Market Worth $10.5 Billion by 2028." www.marketsandmarkets.com/PressReleases/smart-advisor.asp.

Marketsandmarkets.com. Updated on March 3, 2023. www.marketsandmarkets.com/Market-Reports/internet-of-things-market-573.html?gclid=EAIaIQobChMIgdiclLCa_gIVzQiLCh1MnQDyEAAYAiAAEgKog_D_BwE.

Maverick, J.B. and Reviewed by J.R. Brown. July 13, 2022. "Which Types of Industries Have the Largest Capital Expenditures?" www.investopedia.com/ask/answers/020915/which-types-industries-have-largest-capital-expenditures.asp#:~:text=What%20Is%20an%20Example%20of,a%20factory%20or%20an%20airplane (accessed April 24, 2023).

McKinnon, T. January 11, 2023. "8 Reasons Why Blockbuster Failed & Filed for Bankruptcy." www.indigo9digital.com/blog/blockbusterfailure (accessed April 24, 2023).

McKinsey. July 10, 2019. "Why Do Most Transformations Fail? A Conversation With Harry Robinson." *Video*, 0:16. www.mckinsey.com/capabilities/transformation/our-insights/perspectives-on-transformation.

Mediacorp. 2023a. www.channelnewsasia.com/business/mediacorp-socialhub-platform-brands-social-campaign-influencers-2274966 (accessed April 24, 2023).

Mediacorp. 2023b. www.channelnewsasia.com/mediacorp-digital-network (accessed April 24, 2023).

Mediacorp.sg. 2023. www.mediacorp.sg/corporate/news-release/media-releases/lazada-mediacorp-shoppertainment-content-ecommerce-partnership-12969170 (accessed April 24, 2023).

Niessing, J., B. Henry, and K. Peters. March 2018. "Jaguar Land Rover: Towards a Customer-Centric Organisation—Leveraging Customer Intelligence and Data Analytics for Sustainable Growth." ©INSEAD. https://publishing .insead.edu/case/jaguar-land-rover-towards-a-customer-centric-organisation-leveraging-customer-intelligence-and-data-analytics-sustainable-growth.

Nikkei Asia. April 12, 2017. https://asia.nikkei.com/Business/Finance/DBS-sees-biggestthreat-from-internet-players-like-Alibaba-Tencent (accessed April 24, 2023).

Oh, W.Y. and D. Myer. April 26, 2016. "Netflix: International Expansion." Ivey Publishing. Reprinted with Permission.

Pelow, G. and R.D. Austin. September 13, 2019. *Digital Transformation at GE: What Went Wrong?* Ivey Publishing. Reprinted with Permission.

Pidun, U., M. Reeves, and M. Schüssler. September 27, 2019. "Do You Need a Business Ecosystem?" www.bcg.com/publications/2019/do-you-need-business-ecosystem (accessed April 24, 2023).

Pluralsight. January 17, 2023. "Pluralsight's Top Tech Skills for 2023." www .pluralsight.com/blog/teams/top-tech-skills-2023.

Porter, M.E. and J.E. Heppelmann. November 2014. "How Smart, Connected Products Are Transforming Competition." *Harvard Business Review*, p. 8.

Prabhu, A. December 2018. "Business Impact of Digital Transformation Technologies." *Udemy Course.*

Prabhu, A. October 2020. "Digital Strategy: Transform Your business." *Udemy Course.* www.udemy.com/course/digital-strategy/?instructorPreviewMode =guest.

Prabhu, A. December 2020. "5G Fundamentals: A High Level Overview of 5G Cellular Technology."

Ransbotham, S., D. Kiron, P. Gerbert, and M. Reeves. October 2017. "Reshaping Business With Artificial Intelligence: Closing the Gap Between Ambition and Action." *MIT Sloan Management Review*, p. 8.

Rao, V.D. and R. Speculand. November 15, 2021. "How DBS Became the 'World's Best Bank.'" https://knowledge.insead.edu/economics-finance/how-dbs-became-worlds-best-bank.

Restrepo, S. and E. Ojomo. Spring 2022 issue. "Shifting From B2B to B4B Can Build a More Sustainable Business." *MIT Sloan Management Review.*

Sawhney, M. and P. Goodman. May 26, 2022. "Nike: Tiptoeing Into the Metaverse." Northwestern Kellogg School of Management. Reprinted with Permission.

Segran, E. 2018. "Here's Why Nobody Wants to Buy Birchbox, Even After VCs Spent $90M." www.fastcompany.com/40567670/heres-why-nobody-wants-to-buy-birchbox-even-after-vcs-spent-90m (accessed April 24, 2023).

Shapiro, R.D. September 12, 2013. "Process Analysis." *Core curriculum: Operations Management*, p. 3. Harvard Business Publishing.

Share Now Website. 2023. www.share-now.com/ (accessed April 24, 2023).

Sinha, P., D. Sahay, A. Shastri, and S.E. Lorimer. September 2022. "How to Digitalize Your Sales Organization." *Harvard Business Review*. Reprinted with permission.

Statista.com. 2023. www.statista.com/outlook/dmo/digital-advertising/worldwide (accessed April 24, 2023).

Sull, D., S. Turconi, and S. Zanjani. March 2022. "Burberry's Digital Strategy." *London Business School*. Reprinted with Permission.

Tarver, E., Reviewed by T. Brock, and Fast checked by P. Rathburn. December 22, 2022. "Corporate Culture Definition, Characteristics and Importance." www.investopedia.com/terms/c/corporate-culture.asp (accessed April 24, 2023).

The Wall Street Journal. 2023. "The Best and Worst Countries for Business." https://graphics.wsj.com/table/DoingBusiness (accessed April 24, 2023).

Torres. J. 2019. "Sephora vs. Birchbox: Winning Through Digital Retaliation." https://d3.harvard.edu/platform-digit/submission/sephora-vs-birchbox-winning-through-digital-retaliation/ (accessed April 24, 2023).

Training Industry. 2023. "The 70-20-10 Model for Learning and Development." https://trainingindustry.com/wiki/content-development/the-702010-model-for-learning-and-development/ (accessed April 24, 2023).

Tvasta, 2023. "India's First 3D Printed House." https://tvasta.construction/projects (accessed April 24, 2023).

Uduu, O. and K. Kareem. December 29, 2022. "Top 5 Fastest-Growing Sectors and Slowest-Growing Sectors in Q3 2022." www.dataphyte.com/latest-reports/top-5-fastest-growing-sectors-and-slowest-growing-sectors-in-q3-2022/.

Van Alstyne, M.W., G.G. Parker, and S.P. Choudary. April 2016. "Pipelines, Platforms, and the New Rules of Strategy." *Harvard Business Review*, p. 5.

Venkatraman V. February 2017. *The Digital Matrix: New Rules for Business Transformation Through Technology*. LifeTree.

Wattpad.com. 2023. https://company.wattpad.com/archives/2019-4-23-wattpad-and-mediacorp-partner-to-bring-singapore-stories-from-written-word-to-national-screens (accessed April 24, 2023).

werbackspace.com 2023. www.werbackspace.com/digital-advertising-spending-compared-to-traditional-marketing/ (accessed April 24, 2023).

Wikipedia. 2023a. "Birchbox." https://en.wikipedia.org/wiki/Birchbox (accessed April 24, 2023).

Wikipedia. 2023b. "GPT-3." https://en.wikipedia.org/wiki/GPT-3 (accessed April 24, 2023).

Wikipedia. 2023c. "Search Engine Optimization." https://en.wikipedia.org/wiki/Search_engine_optimization (accessed April 24, 2023).

World Economic Forum. January 16, 2023a. "5 Ways We Can Develop the Digital Skills Our Economy Needs." www.weforum.org/agenda/2023/01/5-ways-develop-digital-skills-davos2023/ (accessed April 24, 2023).

World Economic Forum. February 6, 2023b. "What Is Generative AI? An AI Explains." www.weforum.org/agenda/2023/02/generative-ai-explain-algorithms-work/.

www.dbs.com/livemore/sparks/index.html.

www.digiculum.com/ (accessed April 24, 2023).

XR Today. March 15, 2022. "What Can You Do in the Metaverse?" www.xrtoday.com/virtual-reality/what-can-you-do-in-the-metaverse/.

YouTube Video. October 22, 2012. "2D Animated Explainer Video for Freshdesk—Gamify Your Helpdesk." www.youtube.com/watch?v=xDcW9hTyOTo.

YouTube Video. April 5, 2022. "DBS Customer Journeys." www.youtube.com/watch?v=Kgq2LymNTOc.

About the Author

Amit Prabhu has over a decade of corporate experience in Business Management, Strategy, and Consulting. He holds a master's degree in Telecommunications and Networking from the University of Pennsylvania. Besides being a debut Author, he is also a Business Trainer, Speaker, Faculty, Entrepreneur, and Swimming Coach. *Explorer* and *Teacher* are the two words that describe him vividly. He lives in Stockholm, Sweden with his wife and a son.

Index

Letters '*f*' and '*t*' after locators indicate figures and tables, respectively